EVERYTHING
YOU NEED TO WRITE
GREAT ESSAYS
YOU CAN LEARN FROM
WATCHING
MOVIES

EVERYTHING
YOU NEED TO WRITE
GREAT ESSAYS
YOU CAN LEARN FROM
WATCHING
MOVIES

Jay Douglas, Ph.D.

ALPHA

A member of Penguin Group (USA) Inc.

ALPHA BOOKS

Published by the Penguin Group

Penguin Group (USA) Inc., 375 Hudson Street, New York, New York 10014, USA

Penguin Group (Canada), 90 Eglinton Avenue East, Suite 700, Toronto, Ontario M4P 2Y3, Canada (a division of Pearson Penguin Canada Inc.)

Penguin Books Ltd., 80 Strand, London WC2R 0RL, England

Penguin Ireland, 25 St. Stephen's Green, Dublin 2, Ireland (a division of Penguin Books Ltd.)

Penguin Group (Australia), 250 Camberwell Road, Camberwell, Victoria 3124, Australia (a division of Pearson Australia Group Pty. Ltd.)

Penguin Books India Pvt. Ltd., 11 Community Centre, Panchsheel Park, New Delhi—110 017, India

Penguin Group (NZ), 67 Apollo Drive, Rosedale, North Shore, Auckland 1311, New Zealand (a division of Pearson New Zealand Ltd.)

Penguin Books (South Africa) (Pty.) Ltd., 24 Sturdee Avenue, Rosebank, Johannesburg 2196, South Africa

Penguin Books Ltd., Registered Offices: 80 Strand, London WC2R 0RL, England

International Standard Book Number: 978-1-61564-107-9
Library of Congress Catalog Card Number: 2010919336

13   12   11   8   7   6   5   4   3   2   1

Interpretation of the printing code: The rightmost number of the first series of numbers is the year of the book's printing; the rightmost number of the second series of numbers is the number of the book's printing. For example, a printing code of 11-1 shows that the first printing occurred in 2011.

Printed in the United States of America

Note: This publication contains the opinions and ideas of its author. It is intended to provide helpful and informative material on the subject matter covered. It is sold with the understanding that the author and publisher are not engaged in rendering professional services in the book. If the reader requires personal assistance or advice, a competent professional should be consulted.

The author and publisher specifically disclaim any responsibility for any liability, loss, or risk, personal or otherwise, which is incurred as a consequence, directly or indirectly, of the use and application of any of the contents of this book.

Trademarks: All terms mentioned in this book that are known to be or are suspected of being trademarks or service marks have been appropriately capitalized. Alpha Books and Penguin Group (USA) Inc. cannot attest to the accuracy of this information. Use of a term in this book should not be regarded as affecting the validity of any trademark or service mark.

Most Alpha books are available at special quantity discounts for bulk purchases for sales promotions, premiums, fund-raising, or educational use. Special books, or book excerpts, can also be created to fit specific needs.

For details, write: Special Markets, Alpha Books, 375 Hudson Street, New York, NY 10014.

To Penny
(with a tip of the hat to Claudia, who insulted my writing
when I was fifteen and inspired me to prove her wrong)

Contents

Introduction

According to independent research studies by both the College Board and the University of California, a student's writing skills—not math, reading, or SAT scores—are the single best predictor of success in the first year of college. Don't be surprised. Consider the qualities good writers share: creativity, effective communication, research, critical thinking, persistence, and attention to detail. What teacher, professor, or employer wouldn't find value in someone who is competent in all those areas?

Yet when most students compile their lists of favorite activities, writing weighs in somewhere south of a tonsillectomy performed by their Great-Aunt Edna. If you're in that category, there are five things you need to know:

- You are not alone.

- It's not your fault.

- Your situation is not hopeless.

- Every time you watch a movie, you are learning to write better.

- No, I'm not kidding about that last point.

To understand completely, you'll have to read this book—preferably after you buy it—but here's the general idea. The process behind writing an essay, term paper, Ph.D. dissertation, short story, newspaper article, or novel is about the same as the process of making a Hollywood movie. Both writing and filmmaking require preparation time, production time, and finishing-up time. Hollywood calls these three phases pre-production, production, and post-production, respectively.

In filmmaking, these three phases can span a period of years. The most visible part, the glamorous part, is the production phase, with the sets, the crew, the equipment, and the stars. Yet shooting the film consumes only a few weeks out of the filmmaking process. Ask Steven Spielberg, Kathyrn Bigelow, or James Cameron what they are doing during the rest of the time and they'll undoubtedly reply, "I'm making a movie." Filmmakers understand that they don't have to be capturing images on film to be involved in the filmmaking process.

As a writer, focusing solely on putting words on paper is a bit like a filmmaker focusing solely on filming and not bothering to secure the right props or have the sets built or hire all the actors or add music and sound effects to the finished product. Both filmmaker and writer will be unprepared and disorganized. They'll lose sight of the big picture (no pun intended) as they fiddle with the details. In the end, both will feel tired, angry, frustrated, and stressed out. If you're that filmmaker, you'll be looking for a new line of work. If you're that writer, you'll hate what you're writing. You'll hate your teachers, your parents, your friends, and anyone connected with what you're writing. If you're writing about a person, you'll hate him or her, too. Focusing solely on the words-on-paper part is what's made you rail against writing your entire life.

Where did this focus on words come from? As a writer and teacher it hurts me to say this, but you acquired that bad habit in school. It wasn't intentional. Nobody conspired to keep you out of college or cripple your career. Emphasizing the words over the process is an unfortunate side effect of our education system.

While schools teach the mechanics of writing, they rarely address issues such as getting unstuck, writing a first draft, brainstorming, finding where your thesis is hiding, soliciting useful feedback, or telling a story in pictures. Schools don't teach any of that because our education system is geared to teach the parts of writing that can be measured, graded, analyzed, and acted upon.

The part that's missing, the part you don't learn in school, concerns the process of writing. Teaching a process is time intensive. In an era when budget constraints force teachers to deal with more students, shorter classes, and bulging course content, it's not that educators don't know how to teach the writing process, nor that they don't care whether you learn it; educators simply don't have the resources to devote to this critical side of writing. Through no fault of your own, you've learned that writing is all about getting the words down correctly. This is a bit like learning that gourmet cooking is all about arranging food on a plate. To move past the words-on-paper part, you need to discover your personal writing process.

This book can help.

Once you understand how you write, when you write, where you write, and how you work best, you will find your writing experience is more fun, more expressive, and less stressful. Writing may never be your most favorite activity in the whole world, but it will no longer feel like a punishment, an act of self-humiliation, or a skill that perpetually dances out of reach. As you relax into your writing process, you'll see improvements in many areas. You'll have more creative ideas, you'll think before you write, and you'll pay more attention to details. You'll polish your assignments instead of dashing them off the night before they're due. You'll develop these all-important traits not because they are ends in themselves, but because you need them to express what you want to say.

Even if you don't read inside stories about your favorite films online or watch behind-the-scenes bonus material on DVDs, you know more than you think about how films are made and what makes them work. Using that knowledge to improve writing skills is an approach I developed in my 15-plus years of teaching essay writing workshops and college classes. Many of the tips, techniques, and a-ha moments of those years are collected in this book, including advice from students and Hollywood film-makers on applying the principles of Hollywood filmmaking to transform your writing. Read this book, and every time you watch a movie you'll be learning to write more effectively. You might even find your enjoyment of movies increasing, too.

Anyone can learn to write better. You may never be another Toni Morrison or Stephen King. That takes talent, dedication, practice, and more than a little luck. But you can improve how you write and what you write, no matter what your present skill level. If you have the desire, this book, and a few hours a week spent watching movies, can improve both your writing skills and your opportunity for success in school and beyond.

J.D.
Los Angeles
January 2011

How to Use This Book

Think blog posts. That's the way this book is constructed. Each section contains 15 to 20 short entries you might find on a blog instead of in a book. The advantage of a book, though, is now you have something portable, always at the ready; it's something you don't need a WiFi connection or a good 3G signal to read. And, yes, there is something almost respectful in displaying writing about writing in a format larger than a blazer patch.

At the same time, my writing in blog posts instead of long, drawn-out chapters means you get what you want in a style that fits your multitasking world—quick downloads of important information that leave the decision whether to pursue a topic further in your hands, not some absent author's. As such, most of the posts in this book stand by themselves. Use them to solve a specific problem, satisfy your curiosity about a particular topic, or jog your idea-generating faculties. As you read, keep in mind the premise of this book: writing is more than putting words on paper. Writing is a personal process that you can understand and develop in part by watching movies.

Since this book is a collection of what-could-have-been blog posts, each one is followed by some room for you to write a response. Please take advantage of this space. Responding to what you read helps fix the content in your mind, and through your responses, you'll discover secrets about your writing process. This is exactly the information you need to understand how you can write your best and, as such, deserves the permanent inscription.

If you read a post and feel it's just so much pooh pooh, write those comments down, too. Rather than mumble to yourself about how useless a particular post was, lay into what's wrong and write down what the post should have said. In doing so, you'll discover how to take what's in this book and make it work for you. There's nothing wrong with that. Quite the contrary—there's everything right with it.

The only drawback to responding in this book is that, unlike an online blog, your responses don't go anywhere. There's no sharing, no discovering new ideas, no mixing it up with other writers who are working through their writing processes. No worries. Just visit www.pagingDrDoug.com/great_essays to join the conversation with your fellow readers.

Finally, if you have any suggestions for improving this book, or if you'd like to see topics covered in future books or in my podcasts or blogs at the pagingDrDoug website, visit www.pagingDrDoug. com/contact and let me know what's on your mind.

I hope you find this book useful. I'm sure that it will help you discover the pleasures of writing that I've been lucky enough to enjoy over my years as a writer and teacher.

Acknowledgments

Finally, I'd like to thank my wife, Penny, who unselfishly urged me to write this book, knowing full well she'd have to stand bravely at my side as I alternately wrote for hours on end and spent an equal amount of time kicking the furniture in frustration.

One of my wife's observations is that spouses, who are as responsible as the authors for books of this type, receive their thanks way past the point where the average reader has dashed off to the next chapter. If you're one of those readers, you can turn the page now knowing I'll still be married tomorrow.

But I hope you read a bit further.

There are many people who are as responsible for the content of these pages as I am, because their insights and ideas far surpassed my own. If what you read here helps you, they deserve your thanks as much as anyone. Send me a note or contact me through my website at www.pagingDrDoug.com and I'll be sure they know the value of their contributions.

Mistakes, shortcomings, errors, omissions, and anything you find downright unhelpful, that's all me. You can send me a note about that, too, so I can do better next time.

My special thanks to Sam Anderson, Scott Brand, Jeffrey Davis, Greg Dean, Peter Desberg, Laura Dillon, Steve Duncan, Dianne Emerson, Bill Gladstone, Jack Gostl, Shirl Hendryx, Stephen Hopkins, Tom Lipscomb, Tom McLoughlin, Rhonda Rosen, J. D. Ryan, Alex and Judy Singer, Laurie Swanson, Bryna Weiss, and Jeffrey Wynne.

I owe a special debt of gratitude to Kathleen Rushall, my agent at Waterside Productions, who proved herself more than prescient when she told me not to worry, someone would publish this book. She made it sound like a foregone conclusion, though I'm sure she picked up a gray hair or two making it seem that way. Kathleen teamed me up with Randy Ladenheim-Gil, my editor at Alpha Books, and together they made this book possible. Randy immediately embraced the project as if she wrote it herself, and went out of her way to make publishing this book more like a social event than a job. In ways I'll never understand, Randy managed to overcome my determination to immortalize in print a slew of writing blunders without ever raising her voice or sending me an e-mail message full of WORDS IN CAPITAL LETTERS.

The production team at Alpha Books deserves its own shout-out. In this age of point-click-done technology, it's easy to forget that turning a manuscript into a book takes an enormous amount of time, dedication, and attention to detail. My thanks to Megan Douglass, Kayla Dugger, and Jaime Julian Wagner for making it all happen.

Thanks, too, to all my high school workshop and college students and to those students I worked with in individual coaching sessions. Directly or indirectly, they helped shape the material you're about to read. Watching them develop an appreciation for writing was personally rewarding, too. There's nothing like being surrounded by excited writers to renew your own excitement and provide a source of inspiration on those days when your writing isn't going exactly the way you planned.

As if it ever does.

Pre-Production

Pre-production is the first phase of moviemaking—one every self-respecting working director learns to master if he plans to continue being a self-respecting working director. According to Stephen Hopkins, who has 20 years' experience directing both feature films and television, "Pre-production lets me work out the mundane details I need to tell my story. Things like whether an actor needs a shirt pocket to hold a piece of paper, what needs to be on the table in a bar scene, or where the furniture goes so it won't get in the way of the characters. These are things you don't want to deal with during shooting."

No Hollywood director would ever dream of grabbing a camera and shooting a multi-million-dollar film without months of preparation that includes visualizing the story he's about to tell and working out the mundane details so he can tell it. Yet thousands of students tackle their essays—their equally important productions—with barely a nod to any kind of pre-production work.

What goes into an essay's pre-production phase is exactly what goes into pre-production for a film: visualizing the story and assembling the pieces—the raw materials—needed to write the essay. The only difference is that writers approach pre-production in reverse order: raw materials first, visualization second. Directors, after all, start with a script that lays out the story, characters, events, and locations. Writers start with a prompt, and before they can visualize their essays, they have to develop the content.

Hopkins completes his pre-production with cast, crew, shooting script, sets, locations, storyboards, stunt people, editors, assistants, equipment, and budgets all in place. He has visualized the film in his mind and done all he can to prepare himself to move forward with speed and deliberation in the production phase, when he actually shoots his film.

When you have completed your pre-production, you will have amassed far more information than you need (as a result of your research), a visual idea of what your essay looks like, and, most importantly, a thesis that works.

Writing an essay without adequate preparation is akin to shooting thousands of feet of film and hoping to find a movie someplace in the results. Any experienced director will tell you that you don't make great movies by chance. Any experienced writer will tell you that you don't write great essays by chance, either. The good news is that none of this is going to happen to you, because this section will teach you what to do in pre-production mode.

What Is a Movie?

A movie is a story told in pictures.

True, a movie includes a combination of dialogue, music, and—sometimes—text (think of the beginning of the *Star Wars* episodes). But watch a movie with your eyes closed and see (or don't see) if that experience is worth the price of a ticket and popcorn. (You have to keep your eyes closed during the whole movie, not just the scene in which the chainsaw-toting zombie leaps out of the closet.)

A movie is a story told in pictures.

In a well-made film, the pictures so dominate our senses that we forget we are in a theater and find ourselves, instead, in the world of the story. We are on the beach with Tom Hanks, at a wedding reception with Adam Sandler, or lost in space with only HAL as a companion. Imagine what would happen if your teacher, while reading your essay, got lost in its story in the same way.

I heard that and, no, it's not impossible. Just like a film, an essay is a story told in pictures. Granted, no one is going to mistake your three-page essay for a feature film. Nevertheless, you can write an essay that arouses your reader's curiosity, pulls her in, and carries her along on a journey, just like a film, by appealing to your reader's visual sense. Just like a film, you can use visual images to tell your reader a story.

A film's story takes us on a journey from point A to point B. Initially, we tag along to find out what happens next, but in a well-made film, our curiosity gets the better of us. We don't want to know what happens next—we HAVE to know.

Your essay's story starts with a thesis and ends with its proof. That's the journey: from thesis to proof. The arguments you use, the path you take—that's your story, the one you're going to tell in pictures, even though your screen is 11 inches rather than 11 feet high.

In Hollywood, creating pictures from words happens every day. Steven Duncan, who co-created *Tour of Duty* for television, wrote over 50 of its episodes, and is now a professor in the School of Film and Television at Loyola Marymount University, said, "I have to see a film or television episode in my head. If I'm writing about two people in a room, I see the people, the furniture, and the color of the walls. Then I write it down. I've found that if I see what I'm writing about, the person who reads my script sees it, too."

What Duncan says about screenwriting is true for all writing. All writing—including essays, papers, and reports—is about telling a story visually. Like a film, your essay will tell a story with pictures. Those pictures start with words—your words.

Post a reply: _____

_____

_____

_____

Three Things You Must Do in Pre-Production

Michael Moore and Sasha Baron Cohen are magicians. They create films that seemingly materialize out of nowhere. They walk into a store, an office, or a church, and amazing events transpire. We're fortunate the camera was pointed in the right direction. Heck, we're fortunate the camera was there at all. How envious other filmmakers must be; while they slave over scripts, storyboards, casts, and crews, Moore and Cohen are able to crank their cameras and, as if by magic, a film happens.

Like all magic, however, the secret is in the preparation. Not only are Moore and Cohen astute students of human nature, they research their subjects, brainstorm situations, discuss camera coverage, and map out strategies for every response they can imagine. You can be sure that when one of them walks into the frame, he has a good idea of where the film is going and what he has to do to move it there.

The real magic is the way Moore and Cohen make their films look spontaneous, the way they make the story flow as if they had total control over all the situations. Their execution is so flawless at times that their films generate controversy over whether some scenes were staged. Their secret is your secret, too.

Your three most important jobs during pre-production are research, research, and research. Year after year, teachers encounter students who grab their pens and believe that if they just begin writing, something wonderful will happen. They end up frustrated and disappointed. They become angry at their teachers, angry at their assignments, and angry at writing, citing the experience as yet another example of why they can't write. Their essays and papers reflect these feelings and, since how a writer feels about what he writes is how his readers feel about what they read, his readers take away a sense of disappointment and anger instead of interest, confidence, and excitement. When the reader is a teacher or college admissions representative, the consequences of these feelings are sadly predictable.

Danny Simon, the late brother of playwright Neil Simon, once said that the more you know, the more you can write. Simon's words warrant attention. He is one of the fathers of the classic American sitcom. Virtually every actor, writer, and producer working in a sitcom today owes the food on his or her table to Simon. So you might want to scribble down his words and put them where you can see them when you start pre-production:

The more you know, the more you can write.

I brought this up in a writing class once, and one of my students said, "I always find two or three references I can use in my paper." You can imagine the look on his face when I told him that was a good beginning.

"Well, how many do I need?" he asked.

"As many as it takes until you feel you know more about your topic than anybody on Earth," I said. You can imagine how he looked at me then. Probably the way you're looking at this book. What if your teacher is a recognized expert who's written books on the topic of your essay? How can you compete with that?

You don't have to.

Even an expert doesn't remember everything he or she knows about a topic. Remind that expert of something she's forgotten, or express something she knows in a different or interesting way, and you've made a fan for life. If you can't come up with something revolutionary, come up with something surprising.

This is why the three most important tasks in pre-production are research, research, and research; and this is why pre-production is often the longest part of the writing process.

Post a reply: _____

_____

_____

_____

Unsung Heroes

Fast-forward 5, 10, 15 years. You've graduated from college. You've built up no small degree of expertise in your chosen field, the one you studied as an undergraduate, the one in which you now hold an advanced degree, the one in which you've worked all your professional life.

You show up for work Monday through Friday—and perhaps on weekends—with your notes and papers, sleeves rolled up, computer loaded with the software tools you've learned to make dance under your fingers.

You show up for work and nobody comes calling.

There are no phone calls, no e-mail messages, and no hits on your Facebook page. Eight hours later you roll down your sleeves, pack your bag, and return home. Believe it or not, there's a name for this special kind of job and its special kind of hell.

It's called research librarian.

Most public libraries and many school libraries have research librarians. These people are professionals, with degrees in library science, whose expertise comes in ferreting out information.

They are like Google with pulses.

While search engines are impressive tools when your query can be reduced to a few keywords, research librarians are the unsung heroes of essay writing. They are there for queries you can't explain to Google but that make perfect sense to another person, especially one trained in connecting the dots between "It's sort of like …" and a bibliography. They are also lonelier than Mrs. What's-her-name—you know the teacher I'm talking about—must have been while all her friends were at the senior prom.

Rhonda Rosen, Head of Media and Access Services at Loyola Marymount University's William H. Hannon Library, said, "Students rarely come to us when researching a topic. They seem to think if they can't find it using Google, the information doesn't exist.

"The sad thing is we have access to specialized databases with not necessarily more information than the Internet but more reliable information for students."

Rosen also said that so few people ask research librarians for assistance that when you do, you unleash an enthusiasm you can't imagine. Try it. You'll have that librarian's full attention, interest, and desire.

"Send us more students," research librarians tell teachers at conventions, during library tours, and in casual conversations. "Send us more students," they write in their blogs. With this post, I'm doing my job as a writer and a teacher.

I'm sending them you.

Post a reply: _____

_____

_____

_____

Wicked-Pedia

One of the staples of the detective movie is the anonymous tip. The hero, mired in a web of deception, receives a phone call, a letter, or a note in his laundry pointing him in the direction that ultimately leads to the unraveling of the mystery.

Notice that the tip itself never contains the solution to the crime. Like the cryptic "Follow the money" admonition from Deep Throat in the Watergate-era thriller *All the President's Men,* the tip only suggests a direction. The hero must put the pieces together.

As essay writers, we have our own source of anonymous tips: Wikipedia. Just as in the movies, Wikipedia can be an excellent source of information. Or Wikipedia can degenerate into Wicked-Pedia—not derived from the British wicked, as in "wicked good," but *The Wizard of Oz* wicked: mean, cruel, and containing little redeeming value. Just as in the movies, we need to approach Wikipedia tips cautiously.

Anonymity is what transforms Wikipedia from a primary source to an unproven tip. In the movies, the police detective cannot connect the criminal to the crime on the basis of an anonymous tip. Chances are, he cannot even get a search warrant. In essay writing, we can't connect an argument to a thesis on the basis of an anonymous Wikipedia article. We, and the detective, need to present a chain of proof from sources whose accuracy and validity can be independently judged.

Not long ago, a graduate student investigating the nature of Wikipedia authors discovered that the Wikipedia pages for several international corporations were authored and diligently updated from computers AT THOSE CORPORATIONS. A casual visitor browsing those articles would have no idea these Wikipedia pages were stealth public relations ventures.

The philosophy of Wikipedia—that the collective efforts of a community will ultimately cause an article to reflect that community's collective wisdom—works frequently enough that it poses its own special danger. Juxtaposing reliable and unreliable information gives weight to articles that don't deserve it. It's as if the detective got five anonymous tips that all proved correct. Does that mean the sixth is just as valuable? (If you paid attention in math class, you know the answer to that one. Here's a hint: if you roll a die five times, and each time it comes up two, what are the odds it will come up two on the sixth roll?) Like the detective, we can never take a tip at face value. We all have to do our homework.

It's fine to use Wikipedia as a starting point during pre-production. Read about your topic and pull some interesting or curious ideas from the articles. Look to see what references they mention and how reliable those sources are. Then use search engines, library databases, books, articles in academic journals, and your local research librarian to confirm (or not) the information you gleaned from Wikipedia.

Just a few tips for the detective in you to appreciate.

Post a reply: _____

_____

_____

_____

The First 10 Minutes

Little Miss Sunshine is about a family trying to get its young daughter to California so she can enter a beauty pageant. The film makes sense to audiences because they understand where the characters are going.

That doesn't mean California.

It means that as an audience member you understand what each character is trying to accomplish because something has given you a mental road map of the movie. The characters' desire to get to California is simply the glue that holds the story together.

The classic Steven Spielberg film *Jaws* doesn't waste any time inching you toward the edge of your seat. Within 10 minutes, you know a killer shark is terrorizing the small town of Amityville and is about to wreak havoc with the town's Fourth of July celebration. You know that unless Amityville's new police chief and long-time mayor can come to some sort of agreement, there will soon be an awful lot of body parts floating up on the local beaches. And you know that instead of seeing eye to eye, these two will be going at it jaw to jaw.

All this, and you haven't even seen the shark.

That you understand what these movies are about, right from the start, is no accident. Professional screenwriters, directors, and producers know the rules. They learn them from books on screenwriting, in film school classes, and from endlessly studying movies. In the first three pages of a script, the reader knows what the film is about, what point it is making, and what the moral is; by the tenth page, the reader knows who the major characters are, what they want, why they can't (or don't) have it, and what they're going to do about it.

A page of film script represents about a minute of screen time, so if you're sitting in the audience, you know everything you need to know to follow the action in the first 10 minutes of the film.

"It is usually the first 10 minutes of anything I do that my editors and I spend the most time on," says Stephen Hopkins, feature film and television director. With over a dozen films and at least twice that many television episodes under his belt, Hopkins has seen more than his share of first 10 minutes. "It's the setup," he says about this crucial part of a film. If it's not clear, if the audience isn't involved by that time, the rest of the film doesn't matter.

Here's a secret you won't read in writing textbooks: think of your thesis as your first 10 minutes.

A good thesis, among other things, tells the reader everything she needs to know to follow you through your essay: what you're going to prove, where you're starting from, and how you plan to reach your destination. Your reader assumes that every sentence of your essay advances her along that journey. While your thesis holds your essay together for your readers, it also holds the essay together for you. A good thesis tells you what belongs in your essay and what doesn't—the same way the first 10 pages of a script tell the director what belongs in his film and what doesn't.

How do you write a thesis like that? You begin with three principles.

- An effective thesis is specific. If you're arguing that choco-late ice cream is better than vanilla, your thesis should state why. Maybe you believe chocolate ice cream is more ener-gizing than vanilla ice cream, or more emotionally satisfying, or more manly (or womanly). Put it in your first 10 minutes.

- An effective thesis is nontrivial. One job of an essay is to argue for the validity of your point of view when your point of view is open to debate. Theses such as water is wet, elec-tricity can kill you, or squirrels are members of the snake family (their anatomy, not their behavior) are examples of trivial theses. Their points of view have been scientifically, socially, or academically resolved. Unless your essay provides conclusive new evidence to the contrary, there's nothing left to argue. Your reader need not read past the end of your first sentence. Starting your essay with a trivial thesis is akin to starting a movie at the end. Both the movie and your essay are over before they begin.

- An effective thesis argues for only one side of an issue. While *Little Miss Sunshine* was a film about a family trying to win a beauty pageant, the film argued for the value of acceptance and strong family relationships. While there are dozens of different ways of looking at families and their dynamics, *Little Miss Sunshine* took a stand on one of them, inviting you to view your family from a different perspective. That's another job of an essay: to make the reader view an issue in a different way. You do that in your essay the same way the director and writer did it in *Little Miss Sunshine*. You take a stand and you don't waver from it.

Formulating an effective thesis is the most important job you have during pre-production.

Post a reply: _____

_____

_____

_____

Find a Thesis, You Can

It's time to write your essay. You sit down at your desk, pen in hand or keyboard at the ready. You read the prompt. "What was the significance of George Washington's victory over Hessian soldiers in the Battle of Trenton?" Confidently you write your thesis statement. I say confidently because you remember the words Yoda spoke to Luke in *Return of the Jedi:* "Already know you, that which you need." You write, "The significance of George Washington's victory over Hessian soldiers in the Battle of Trenton was …" Already know you, that which you need—George Washington, a victory, Hessian soldiers, Battle of Trenton, significant. Everything was waiting for you in the prompt.

If you learned to create a thesis statement by rephrasing the prompt, it's best you heed Yoda's advice from *The Empire Strikes Back:* you must unlearn what you have learned.

The technique of finding a thesis statement in the prompt works well for test questions disguised as essays because these so-called essays are designed to measure what you remember, not what you feel, about a topic. The method fails miserably when you encounter a prompt that begins with a general observation about a topic and goes on to ask for your opinion. Turning that kind of prompt around results in a writing session that can leave you feeling as though you've been sliced in two by a lightsaber.

Pull yourself together. There is a technique for creating a thesis statement for even the most challenging prompts. Ready, are you?

Perhaps the most difficult prompt you'll ever encounter is one for a college application personal statement. These prompts are deliberately and excruciatingly vague and range from the reality-twisting

"If you could have dinner with any person, living or dead, real or imaginary, who would it be, and why?" to the unhelpful "Tell us something about yourself." Trying to write an essay by working with the literal prompt—that is, by looking for a thesis statement in the prompt—is ... well ... see for yourself.

Grab a sheet of paper and answer this prompt: tell me about your school. Spend no more than five minutes, then proceed to the next paragraph. (It's important that you do this activity and not simply read about it.)

Put that sheet of paper aside. On another sheet, answer this prompt: tell me about a teacher you hate. Write about that special teacher whose very name makes your face flush and your finger-nails ache. (If you prefer, you can write about a teacher you admire, but for this activity hate, strong distaste, or total frustration works better.) Why do you feel this way about this teacher? What habits or behaviors does this teacher exhibit that make you cringe? How do these behaviors make you feel? What would you like to do about it? Begin writing.

Now let's match up these two short essays. The essay about your teacher probably contains passion and emotion. Your writing is specific. You have names, times, places, and details. Your feelings are undoubtedly well represented, and they unmistakably infuse your writing with energy.

By comparison, your description of your school is flat. It leans on facts rather than emotion and generalities rather than specifics. Chances are, your essay is little more than a glorified list, and that list contains five or fewer items. You most likely experienced little fun writing about your school and frequently asked yourself,

"What does this guy want?" Does any of this sound familiar? Does any of it sound like experiences you've had working on homework assignments? Why did this happen? What made your two pieces of writing so markedly different?

There's no Jedi magic at work here, although you may have guessed there is some trickery.

The first prompt—write about your school—is a slight variation of "tell me about yourself," and was meant to be extremely vague. Write WHAT about your school? Mentally, you ran through a list of topics: size, location, types of classes, facilities. For lack of any other guidance, you put these facts in your writing.

The second prompt was as focused as the first one was broad: write about a SPECIFIC person and a SPECIFIC emotion. Then there were those questions. Remember them? WHO is this teacher? WHAT does he do? HOW does that make you feel? WHAT would you like to do about it? These weren't ordinary questions, either; they're derived from the famous Five W's of journalism—who, what, when, where, and why—and their close personal friend, how. Each question helped you focus your attention on a particular aspect of your feelings.

Viewed in this light, your writing results are easy to explain. When you tried to write about a general topic, the results ranged from a weak, unsatisfying few paragraphs (and an equally unsatisfying writing experience) to no paragraphs at all, just a list. Given a specific topic and some techniques for narrowing down the prompt even further, the result was an energized, emotional, even passionate piece of writing. Notice that both of your short essays are suitable responses to the prompt to "tell me about your school." If you were turning one essay in for a grade, which one would it be?

Had Yoda been a writing coach, he probably would have offered you this admonition:

Better than general, specific is.

In pre-production, being specific helps you fashion your thesis, but being specific is so important in all three essay-writing phases that you might want to jot this down and put it someplace where you can see it while you write:

Better than general, specific is.

When you find yourself up against a general prompt, your first task is to turn that prompt into something specific. In another post (see "Brainstorming," page 20), you can learn about using brainstorming to do just that. Meanwhile, if you need to be convinced that this technique is one you simply have to attend to during pre-production, reread your two short essays.

See which one would make Yoda proud.

Post a reply: _____

_____

_____

_____

Brainstorming

In an earlier post (see "Find a Thesis, You Can," page 16), I wrote about the need to turn a general prompt into a specific thesis. Since a thesis may very well be the most important outcome of pre-production, here's a one-word strategy for narrowing down a prompt: brainstorm.

Brainstorming is more than a technique for generating ideas; it's a way of developing a feel for your essay starting with only the sketchiest details. Brainstorming is very closely allied to what actors do when they act "in the moment."

You've seen actors acting in the moment; you just didn't realize it. Watch the work of Meryl Streep, Jack Nicholson, Frances McDormand (you must see her performance in *Fargo*), or William H. Macy (you wouldn't know him if you saw him—he's that good) and you'll realize these actors are so in the moment that they ARE the characters they're playing. When the cameras roll, actors who are working in the moment are not on a sound stage under lights and in front of a crew, they are living in the make-believe world the screenwriter and director have created for them. They believe they are the characters they are playing. So do we.

As writers, being in the moment can work for us. If we're writing about ancient Rome, we're there. When we look around, we don't see our bookcase, desk, and computer; we see aqueducts, marble statues, and the Coliseum. We don't hear the clicks of the keyboard; we hear the murmur of citizenry or the chanting of crowds. In any other field, behavior like this would be grounds for a psych evaluation. As a writer, this behavior is not only normal, it's desirable. (But let's keep that behavior our little secret.) Discovering details, especially details we didn't know we knew, is exactly what we need to develop a thesis. For many writers, brainstorming is the gateway to writing in the moment. Chances are, brainstorming will prove the same for you.

The next few posts describe some brainstorming techniques my students have used successfully. Experiment with the activities described for each method. If you already use one of them, definitely try out the others. Different methods work better at different times and with different assignments.

After those posts, there's one that discusses why brainstorming works. You don't need to understand its psychological explanation to use the techniques any more than you need to understand organic chemistry and molecular bonding to drive a car. You might want to read the post, though, because it will help you understand that many of the experiences you have while writing—such as feeling blocked, feeling uncreative, or feeling dumb—have NOTHING to do with being blocked, uncreative, or dumb. These feelings are a normal part of the writing process and are shared by writers everywhere, including the pros.

Experiment with the brainstorming activities and see which ones work best for you.

Post a reply: _____

_____

_____

_____

Make a List

Making a list is the simplest brainstorming technique there is. You can turn to it when your idea-creating mechanism needs a quick jolt. Try it out now using this prompt for practice: What person in your life has influenced you the most?

For the next 10 minutes, jot down any ideas the prompt inspires. There are only two rules. First, you cannot think about whether or not to write down a thought. If it comes into your head, you MUST put it on the page. Second, you cannot edit your list. Once an item is on your list, it stays there. In fact, you cannot reread your list. (This is rule two and a half.) Simply keep moving forward with more thoughts.

You may find the hardest part of this activity is the no-thinking rule. Most thinking occurs when your pencil or typing fingers aren't moving. So keep them in action. That means if you can't think of something on target, write down something off target. After all, you're just coming up with ideas here, and the concepts of on target and off target are murky to say the least. Begin your list-making now. After at least 10 minutes, when it seems you've exhausted the topic, continue with the next paragraph.

Look over your list. It probably contains your parents, perhaps your grandparents, a sibling, maybe a few more close relatives. There's nothing wrong with that. However, if that's all your list contains, keep going for another 10 minutes. Brainstorming works in different ways for different people, but one common characteristic is that obvious ideas come out first. Part of the beauty of brainstorming is that it can help you tap into the nonobvious ideas. Stopping when your page appears to be covered with exciting thoughts, but is mostly a gathering place for the obvious, is one of the most oft-cited reasons for abandoning brainstorming. "I would have thought of these anyway," students say. "Why go through all this nonsense to get to the same result?" Of course, they're right. Brainstorming is nonsense—if you stop too soon. So if your list contains only the obvious influences, press on to the nonobvious ones.

Once you've listed yourself into a state of brain ache, look over your list and circle what YOU BELIEVE are the best three items on it. The meaning of "best" is entirely up to you. If you think a choice deserves to be circled, circle it. If you simply MUST circle more than three, sorry; whittle down your choices.

Out of those three, which choice do YOU BELIEVE is the best? Again, the parameters of the choice are yours. The lone survivor is the one to use in answering the prompt. Your relationship to this person is the focus of your thesis. Can you fashion that thesis now? Odds are you can. (Don't just think about it; do it.)

Simply by working through a list, you've narrowed down a general prompt into a specific thesis. If you were writing an essay in response to this prompt, you would now know who you were writing about and, more often than not, have a rough idea of the details you'd like to include (see "Find a Thesis, You Can," page 16).

While this list-making activity might be thought of as instant brainstorming (you can do it anywhere, and it doesn't take much time), it can help you tap into ideas you didn't know you knew. Did this happen to you? If not, be patient. Brainstorming is part science and part art. Mastering it takes a little time and practice. The more you brainstorm, the better ideas you come up with. While doing this activity, a former student wound up writing about a job she had with a large company. She didn't want to write about the people at the company; she wanted to write about how the company itself had changed her life. A second student asked her how she came up with that, and the first student replied that the company was a corporation and that a corporation is considered a person under the law. So, she argued, she WAS writing about a person. Her interpretation of the word "person" was inventive, and so was her essay.

Such is the power of list-making.

Post a reply: _____

_____

_____

_____

Freewriting

Freewriting is just what it sounds like. Using pencil and paper or your computer, you just write. You write whatever comes into your head. You write nonstop for 20 minutes. It's no more complicated than that. Freewriting is, however, one of the best-kept brainstorming secrets in America. Most students have never used it, possibly because the thought of writing for 20 minutes sounds intimidating—or possibly because, when they try it, they get results like this:

> i want to write about my father only i'm not sure what i want to say about him. everything i think of sounds really ordinary and there's more to say about him that's not ordinary and i don't want him sounding in this essay like every other father because then i shouldn't be writing about him and i should find someone else to write about and i don't want to write about that because i think i don't love him and that makes him sound mean and he wasn't mean i think he thought he was doing the right thing and we did go for walks when he would tell my brother that he couldn't come along because he was too young to walk the dog and so he would take me out with the dog and i know it was because he wanted to spend time with me and that was nice but then he would turn around the next day and tell me i couldn't go to the baseball game because my mother didn't want me riding home on the bus alone at night and i don't know why he took my mother's side all the time

It's hard to admit to yourself, let alone anyone else, that you spent valuable time writing THAT. The lack of punctuation and capitalization aside, it's not exactly a piece of work you'd want to stake your GPA on. In a few paragraphs, you'll understand why these ramblings are so useful. First, though, let's see how freewriting is done.

People who are new to freewriting begin by asking the same question: "Where do I start?" Even with permission to write ANYTHING they want, that first sentence seems particularly elusive. Fortunately, and this is one of the delights of freewriting— your choice of a first sentence doesn't matter.

That sounds counterintuitive, but the freewriting experience of thousands of practitioners confirms that where you start or what first sentence you write typically bears little resemblance to where you wind up—or what you discover along the way. Rather than inventing a new first sentence every time, you can begin with something like, "I want to write about _____" and fill in the blank with a word or phrase suggested by the prompt.

If you read the post on list-making (see "Make a List," page 22), then you already know the two rules of that brainstorming activity. They apply to freewriting, too. You cannot think about what you write. If an idea comes into your head, you MUST write it down. Once a word is on the page, it stays on the page. You cannot edit what you write. How do you know when you're thinking? You stop writing. When you're brainstorming, thinking and writing are mutually exclusive.

(Another freewriting rule is that you never, EVER have to show your freewriting to anyone. If a friend or relative asks to see what you wrote, simply say, "This is for me." Repeat as necessary until your inquisitive acquaintance gets the message.)

What do you do if you find yourself stuck with nothing to write about? Since the heart of freewriting is writing whatever is in your head, if you feel stuck, write "I feel stuck," or words to that effect. Keep writing it until something else takes its place. One writing student wrote, "I have nothing to write about" for two pages before her mind moved on. It's fine if you have an entire freewriting session of "I feel stuck." Your brain is working on new ideas; they're just not ready yet.

After 20 minutes, read what you've written. Most of it, like the previous example, will be ... let's call it unique. Once in a while, though, you'll find something that surprises you, delights you, or makes you smile. Underline it. Then go back and review what you've underlined. If the preceding freewriting were yours and was based on a prompt about someone who influenced your life, you might have selected the following:

- he would tell my brother that he couldn't come along because he was too young to walk the dog and so he would take me out with the dog and i know it was because he wanted to spend time with me

- i couldn't go to the baseball game because my mother didn't want me riding home on the bus alone at night and i don't know why he took my mother's side all the time

There are a few potential essay topics here. One is the idea that your brother was too young to walk the dog. How did your relationship with your brother and your dog influence you? Did the responsibility for walking the dog leave you feeling important or put upon? Did you have to walk the dog while your brother played with his friends? How did that change your life growing up?

Another topic involves the walks with your father. What happened on those walks that affected your life? What did you talk about when there was no one else around? Did you confide your secrets? What did you learn about your father, or sharing secrets, that affects you to this day?

A third topic has to do with your mother feeling you were too young to ride the bus home from a baseball game. Were you too young? Were you trying to show her you were a grown-up? Did you succeed? How did the attempt affect the rest of your life?

Notice that only one of the topics has to do with your father, which is where the freewriting began. Unexpected ideas crop up all the time in freewriting, and that's why it's not worth agonizing over what words you use to get started. Nor is it worth agonizing over whether your freewriting uncovered anything "good." Often, as in this case, none of your underlined passages will suggest a thesis. Keep freewriting. Pick one topic and use it as the start of another session (though you might want to let your brain rest for a few hours). Which topic? The one that surprises you, delights you, or makes you smile the most—or even a little.

No matter what your topic, be patient. Sometimes the process doesn't seem to work. You write for 20 minutes and find nothing of interest. That's normal. Our brains are crammed full of thought scraps that have to come out before you get to the good stuff. Once those scraps are out of the way, you're closer to those creative ideas. And on those days when the freewriting clicks, the results are amazing.

Post a reply: _____

_____

_____

_____

Clustering

List-making and freewriting (see "Make a List," page 22; and "Freewriting," page 25) are written forms of brainstorming. If you're more of a visual person, you may prefer clustering because it relies on images more than words. Even words-on-paper people may find clustering helpful at times. The only way to know for sure is to give it a try.

Suppose the prompt for your essay is "What person in your life has influenced you the most?" (This is a common prompt for personal statements.) Begin the clustering session by writing down a word (or phrase) suggested by the prompt. Write the word in the center of a piece of paper (sorry, computers are not clustering friendly) and draw a circle around the word.

Next, write down a second word suggested by the first. Draw a circle around the second word and connect the two circles with lines and arrows.

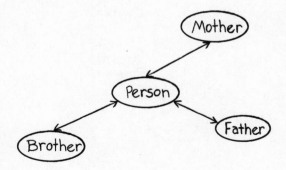

Repeat the process. Put down a word suggested by either of the two words on the page. Circle it, and connect it with lines and arrows to the word that suggested it. Keep going. After a while, your page will look something like this.

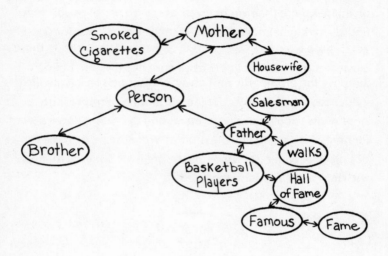

Since this is a brainstorming activity, brainstorming rules apply: no thinking, no editing. You're thinking when your pencil stops moving, so if you find you're stuck for a word, keep your pencil in play by darkening existing circles, lines, and arrows.

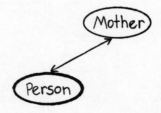

Cluster for about 20 minutes, put the page aside for a little while, and then take a look at the whole page for the first time. Invariably, you'll find that on some parts of the page, the circles seem to cluster together (you knew the name clustering came from somewhere). In this example, note what's happening around the word "father."

Look at the words and thoughts in those clusters. What do those clusters suggest? Is there the beginning of a thesis in there? If you're not sure, take one of the thoughts from the cluster and use it as the first word of a new clustering session.

Like the other brainstorming activities in this book, clustering requires the twin P's: practice and patience. Once you get in the rhythm of clustering, though, it can be a highway to thesis ideas you didn't know you had.

One truth you will discover about brainstorming is that it does not often work well under pressure, especially when you are new to the techniques. During pre-production, allow yourself enough brainstorming time. Remember, it might take two or three sessions at first to focus in on a thesis. Even brainstorming pros know that ideas don't always arrive on your schedule. Start your brainstorming early so you can relax and enjoy the process.

Post a reply: _____

_____

_____

_____

Why Brainstorming Works

The essence of every great film is conflict. A basic action/ adventure film pits a larger-than-life hero against an even larger-than-life villain. At the heart of romance films is the loving couple who can't stand each other. Horror films employ demons and monsters whose sole purpose is to make life miserable for the peaceful inhabitants of small Midwestern towns (though lately living in a small New England town doesn't guarantee peace and quiet, either).

Conflict is important because the push and pull of characters, both locked in a battle for a mutually exclusive goal, is what drives the film forward. Conflict is so important to storytelling that it's not surprising we find conflict at the heart of the writing process. You might say conflict is built into our brains.

The human brain is split into two halves: a left brain and a right brain. The right brain controls the left side of the body and vice versa. Their responsibilities don't end with physical control. The right brain heads (no pun intended) the department of creative ideas. As a creative type, the right brain is intuitive and nonverbal. It "thinks" with pictures and concepts rather than words. Words, logic, speech, rational thought—those are the province of the left brain. The left brain is in charge of making decisions, handling written and spoken communication, and communicating with the outside world.

When you sit down to write, your right brain generates ideas. Since the right brain has no language facilities, it passes the ideas to the left brain. "Write 'em down," the right brain says.

Ever logical, the left brain looks over the ideas before tossing them out to the universe. "Wait a minute," says the left brain, "you can't be serious about this. This is awful. People will laugh at us."

"Do you think?" says the right brain. "Well, okay. I can come up with something better. That's what I do." Coming up with ideas is not only what the right brain does, it's what the right brain loves to do. In no time, the left brain has another idea on its desk.

"Oh no," says the left brain, "this one is worse than before."

"Fair enough," says the right brain. "I can do better." The left brain's comment on the next idea is unprintable.

We've all experienced this cycle. The right brain comes up with ideas, and the left brain shoots them down. Talk about conflict. Neurons firing, chemicals reacting, thoughts flashing as two equally matched blobs of gelatinous matter battle over … well, they're battling over your essay, your grade, your degree, and your future.

Wow. We've got to see how this turns out.

Act Two isn't quite as interesting. Here is where the right brain, frustrated in its attempts to get an idea—any idea—on the page, calls it quits. Figuratively speaking, the right brain walks out of the movie. It returns to its trailer and refuses to budge. Not even bowls of multicolored M&Ms can coax the right brain back to the set. We have a name for this. No, it's not "star temperament." It's called writer's block. (See what happens when we take the conflict out of the story?)

Writer's block is NOT an inability to write. Writer's block sufferers have no problem writing e-mail messages, shopping lists, Post-It notes, and tweets. Writer's block sufferers have a right brain that's given up in disgust while the movie still has two hours to go.

Brainstorming helps restore order to this conflict by capitalizing on the quality the left brain shares with every good villain: vulnerability.

The left brain abhors repetitive tasks, making boredom our villain's kryptonite. Put the left brain in charge of something monotonous and it eventually loses its focus. Its knees grow weak, its eyes grow fuzzy, and the world starts to swim (that's your left brain, not you). While it's sinking, blinking, and swimming, it's not filtering those right-brain ideas. Instead, those ideas sneak through untouched. The right brain, encouraged that its work is getting an airing, keeps pumping ideas through the pipeline—ideas the left brain dutifully ignores while it is grousing to itself about how bored it is.

All we need, then, are some nice, boring, repetitive tasks. Let's say … oh … drawing circles, lines, and arrows or writing down a rush of words that seem to have no purpose. In other words, brainstorming.

Requiring the left brain to keep those fingers moving, to tend to the mechanics of writing rather than the content of that writing, is the secret behind the brainstorming activities in my earlier posts (see "Make a List," page 22; "Freewriting," page 25; and "Clustering," page 29). As long as the left brain is engaged in this activity, the right brain will sneak its ideas through to the page. This is why those posts went overboard on the importance of nonstop writing or clustering. When your fingers stop working, the left brain is free to meddle once again, and meddle it will. It's in the left brain's contract.

Perhaps you can see why brainstorming often produces surprising results. The right brain not only has a direct line to your memory, it's also quite clever at combining what seem to be unrelated bits of information into new ideas. Your right brain is literally coming up with thoughts you didn't know you thought. Those thoughts hit the page before the left brain even knows they've arrived. You see them for the first time when you read your brainstorming results. You're shocked. Your left brain is shocked. Your right brain returns to its trailer and smirks.

By Act Three, your left brain has been rehabilitated. Say what you will, the left brain is a highly effective editor. Now that it has ideas to work with, the left brain can pick and choose among them. "Most of these are garbage," the left brain says. "But these ideas over here—they're actually quite good."

"Oh, really?" says the right brain, "Because I can do more like that."

And so it does. (Now you know why we often need several brainstorming sessions before we find a thesis idea that clicks.) In the end, boy gets girl, or brain gets brain, and everyone lives happily ever after.

Until the next essay.

Post a reply: _____

_____

_____

_____

It's in the Cards

Chances are, your favorite film began its life as a pile of index cards. In books and in classrooms, laying out a film as a series of index cards is the most often-mentioned technique for organizing a script before it's written. Every scene gets a card that charts the activity and characters in the scene, perhaps along with a few bits of dialogue. It takes 40 to 60 cards to represent a full-length film, but filling out the cards is only the beginning of the process. Screenwriters also juggle the cards, organizing them into a story. "I like to see scenes in order so I can patch them together and get an idea of how the story's going to flow," says Jeff Wynne, a 20-year veteran of film and television writing. For Wynne, laying out scenes also pays another dividend when he sits down to write his script. "I never have to stare at a blank page, because now I've got bits and pieces of the story I know I've got to get to." The index card method of laying out a film is another strategy you can bring to your essay writing.

During your research, jot down information on index cards. Find an interesting quote? Write it on a card. Think of an idea you want to include in your essay? Write it on a card. Inspired by a paragraph you just read? Write it on a card. Have a random thought that MIGHT pertain to your essay? Write it on a card. If what you wrote on the card came from, or was inspired by, another source, such as a book or magazine article, write some identifying information on the back of the card. That way, you can quote the author directly and give her credit.

Toss the cards in a stack and put them someplace safe. It's a good idea not to refer to them during your research. True, you might wind up with several cards containing roughly the same content, but that's your gut telling you the content is important. Not editing your cards during pre-production also means you'll have sufficient raw material to plumb during your production phase.

When you're researched out, take your stack of cards to a large, flat workspace (such as a floor or table) that you can monopolize for a few days. Lay out all your cards and put them in order. What order? Any order you think makes sense. What thoughts need to come first? Move those cards to the top left corner of your work area. See any thoughts that look like they summarize what you want to say? Bottom right. Find those cards with ideas that support the point you want to make (or think you want to make). These cards will fill up the middle of your workspace.

Feel free to move cards around. There is no right place for anything. If a card at the bottom right now seems to belong at the upper left, move it. If you have two cards in the middle of your workspace, swap their positions just to see what happens. Do two cards seem to hold the same thought? Put one on top of the other. Are ideas beginning to flow together? Keep adding cards and moving them around until you feel satisfied—until you can scan the cards from upper left to lower right and recognize the story those cards are telling you.

Although it appears your workspace is covered with index cards, it's actually covered with your essay. It's all right there in front of you, waiting to be turned into the tale you want to tell. By arranging and rearranging them, you'll begin to see just how you'll tell it: what your introduction might be, what your thesis might say, how you will support your argument, what you will pull in to drive your conclusion home. Suddenly, you'll hear the production phase calling your name.

Yes, it sounds like an outline, and in terms of content, it is. Outlines, though, are terribly inflexible. They allow you only two choices for an idea: above or below. Cards are multidimensional. You have above, below, left, right, on top, underneath, overlapping, nearby, and way out there by the bookcase. Outlines are 8½ by 11 inches. On the floor of your bedroom, your cards can span 8½ by 11 FEET.

Grandeur is not the only reason to consider working this way. While you're moving the cards around—and this is an effect that's hard to explain—your essay will seem to come alive, almost as if the cards know where to go. You're not directing them as much as simply supplying the horsepower to get them where they want to be. You might not want to mention this (except to other writers), because at best it sounds as if your bedroom is a giant Ouija board. At worst, it's a downer at job interviews. Nonetheless, you'll soon find yourself staring at your essay. Maybe it's not your final essay, but certainly it's the best idea you have for your essay as pre-production winds down. Don't be surprised if you also discover you can turn around and tell an imaginary listener (another topic to leave out of job interviews) the story of your essay the way a screenwriter can tell a producer the story of his film.

This is one of those adventures in writing that you have to experience to appreciate, let alone believe. If you're not using this method (or something similar) in your research, try it and see what happens.

You might discover that using cards is a good deal.

Post a reply: _____

_____

_____

_____

Write It Down So You Can Write It Down

Once upon a time a friend and fellow writing teacher met a talent agent at a party. You know all those actors you see in films? Their talent agents got them there. (If you don't believe it, ask their talent agents. Just don't ask the actors.) Talent agents match up actors and roles. From this they make a living. Many of them make a four-Mercedes, three-home, one-yacht living.

This talent agent wanted to put my friend in the movies. It's a funny idea because he has terrible camera fright. He can teach a class of a thousand students, but finds the thought of performing in front of a mechanical device with a lone glass eye debilitating. The agent insisted my friend wouldn't have to perform, he'd just have to stand there, because he looked like the perfect absent-minded professor.

Ouch. My friend was outed. He is absent-minded, especially when it comes to his writing. That's why he carries a notebook with him wherever he goes. Everything winds up in that notebook: story ideas, book ideas, opening sentences, interesting or funny lines he overhears, billboard headlines, silly signs, and paragraphs or pages for projects he's working on—or wishes he were working on. Relying on that notebook used to bruise his ego. That's why the talent agent's remarks struck a nerve. Then he learned he wasn't alone.

Most of the successful people, people whose success depends on a constant flow of ideas, record the same sort of information in the notebooks they carry. Some use personal voice recorders. One acquaintance e-mails ideas to herself from her smartphone. Rather than a sign of weakness (or too much partying in their early days), notebooks are membership cards in an exclusive club—the club of people whose stock in trade is ideas.

My friend summed up the other dose of reality he learned in one sentence, written on an index card and posted over his desk:

> Write it down now.

Not remembering your flashes of brilliance has nothing to do with your age, how much sleep you've had, whether you're eating right, or the fact that your father remembers the license plate number of every car he's ever owned. It does, however, have everything to do with your right brain.

Ideas originate in your right brain (see "Why Brainstorming Works," page 32). When it comes to generating ideas, your right brain's attitude suffers from arrested development—the arrest having been made back when you were two or three. At that age, your full-time job was discovering cool new things. You'd find one, ooh and ahh over it for a respectful amount of time—30 seconds to a minute seemed about right—and then bound off to something else. Today, your right brain does the same thing with ideas. It pops off an exciting idea, oohs and ahhs over it, then charges off to something else. Remember the idea? Hey, that's not in the right brain's job description.

Ideas from the right brain can be intense, so you may feel 100 percent certain you'll remember them for the rest of your life. Actually, you'll remember them until the right brain is off on a new adventure. Hence the inscription on that index card that used to hang over my friend's desk:

> Write it down now.

Take his advice. Write it down in the notebook you're going to start carrying. "Whenever I have an idea for something, I write it down and put it in a folder. And whenever I have another idea that relates to the first, I'll put it in the folder, too," says Steven Duncan, professor of screenwriting at Loyola Marymount University in Los Angeles. If you don't like notebooks, take Duncan's advice and start a folder for your writing projects. While you're in pre-production, you're going to come up with ideas for your essay, such as opening sentences, whole paragraphs, arguments, thesis statements, and insights. With that notebook or folder (or smartphone, if you type faster than you write), you'll be ready because you're going to …

Write it down now.

You'll get ideas in the shower, as you fall asleep, when you wake up, in the middle of a movie, and during class. With the notebook, folder, or smartphone you'll capture those ideas for production and post-production because you will …

Write it down now.

Alex Singer, who began his Hollywood directing career in 1961 and went on to direct more hours of television than you were probably allowed to watch while growing up, made this observation about writing: "Writers need to have a rich brew to reach into to use as fodder for their creativity. Great ideas never come from a blank mind." Or from a blank notebook page. That's why, when you get your next great idea, you're going to …

Write it down now.

As a postscript, my friend's ego did succumb to the talent agent's temptation and he went out on a few auditions. He was the bomb, but not in today's sense. He was the bomb in the other sense— your grandparents' sense: the single worst actor in the lot, any way you measured him.

He remembered that, and he didn't have to write it down.

Post a reply: _____

_____

_____

_____

Hiring Your Cast and Crew

Millions of people live in Los Angeles because they want to be in the movies. Some of these people are great. Others have talent and potential. Most have only dreams, and those dreams are destined to remain unfulfilled. Whatever the reason, these people don't have the stuff to make it in the high-stakes world of feature films.

The millions of pages and articles on the web are much like these Angelenos. Some web pages and articles are well researched and well written. The ideas you extract from them enhance your argument and make your essay sparkle. Other web pages have potential but are short on facts. Like inexperienced hopefuls, they can be useful, but will require close scrutiny and supervision. These pages will spark ideas, but you'll still need to search for other sources to shore up what you find. Most web pages, however, are full of dreams—some metaphorically and some literally. Craft and rigor are replaced by assumptions and outright errors. These are the pages that can cripple your production because they don't do their jobs. They fail to provide the verifiable facts and well-reasoned opinions you need to lend credibility to your argument. These are the web pages you don't want anywhere near your essay.

Reputations spread quickly in Hollywood, but checking credentials on the web presents a greater challenge. There are few referral services to help you sort out the desirable sources from the undesirable ones. Showing up in a Google search guarantees nothing. Showing up at the top of a Google search guarantees even less. (If you haven't heard of Google bombing, search for the term and see what I'm talking about. While you're at it, see the post about

Wikipedia: "Wicked-Pedia," page 10.) This doesn't mean you can't do your own reference checking, only that you need to work at it. Here are some tips my students suggest:

- Sites ending in .edu don't automatically provide valid academic content. Many universities offer free web pages to students who then post material that's not well researched. Check the author's credentials. Professors usually have home pages that list their backgrounds, specialties, and publication histories. As a bonus, you may find a list of other writing by the same professors that will help you in your research.

- Look for second sources. A good article cites its sources. Check these out. Are they reputable?

- Look for independent sources. Many bloggers get their information from other bloggers, who in turn get their information from a handful of websites. One blogger makes a post and other bloggers repeat it, often without attribution. Suddenly, it appears as if the information is all over the web (and therefore credible). A reliable site will adhere to the rules of good journalism by verifying information and citing sources.

- Look for sites with reputations to protect. Major news sites, for example, cannot afford to disseminate rumors or inaccurate information. They may not always get the facts right, but they own up to mistakes and correct the record. Nevertheless, always verify what you find on one site with information from an independent second (or third) source.

- Popularity does not translate to accuracy or reliability. Aggregators such as Digg, Google Trends, and Twitter tell you what's hot, but trends can change in minutes. Always think for yourself.

- Use academic databases for online research. Databases such as LexisNexis, Wilson Select, and ProQuest may be available through your school or public library (see "Unsung Heroes," page 8). The content of these databases is drawn from carefully selected sources whose existence rests on their ability to consistently deliver credible, peer-reviewed information.

- Remember, no matter how objective the content of a site appears to be, the content got there through the decisions of people, and people have biases. Reputable sites take steps to minimize this bias (through the use of review committees, for example), but minimize does not mean eliminate. As your essay's author, your job is to look at all sides of your topic and decide for yourself what information to use and what to discard.

Yes, rounding up a cast and crew takes effort. The process is time-consuming. But when your essay is over and the credits roll, when your reader looks over your reference page, you and your reader will both know that you're working with professionals.

Post a reply: _____

_____

_____

_____

I've Got a Question

This post is an exception to the others in this book. It's written in the first person because I couldn't find a clear way of explaining the process involved by describing how someone else might do it. Please bear with me, and remember that the post is here to help you work through the process yourself.

Before you begin your production draft, I'm going to let you in on the secret of writing. I don't know why it's such a secret, but when I talk about it with students, no one seems to have heard it before.

Writing is all about seeing an image in your head and then writing down the words that make your reader see the same image. Not too mysterious, is it? To write well, then, you first have to see in your head the image you want your reader to see (see "Picture This," page 53). The sharper your image, the easier it will be for you to choose the words that will transfer that image to your reader. While it sounds easy in principle, putting it into practice is often challenging.

Here's a method that helps screenwriting students visualize their movies as they write their scripts. It can help you, too. To demonstrate it, I'll answer a typical question you might find as a personal statement prompt on a college application: Describe some incident or event that taught you a lesson. I'll be writing about a lesson I learned one Sunday morning during a walk with my father.

Begin with a simple location and action.

> My father and I were walking along the street with our dog when a man stopped us. He recognized my father as a former basketball player.

Can you see this scene in your mind? Perhaps you can, but only vaguely. Perhaps you see nothing at all. There isn't much for you to go on. I'll fill in some details.

My father and I were walking along the street …

Where was this? We were walking along Kingsbridge Road in the Bronx. This section of Kingsbridge Road was a shopping district, with mom-and-pop neighborhood businesses—drug stores, candy stores, vegetable stands, hardware stores, and toy stores— lining both sides of the street. The street itself was always clogged with buses, taxis, trucks, and cars. On some days, it seemed that everybody in the Bronx was trying to drive along this one stretch of street. Can you see Kingsbridge Road better now?

… with our dog

I can surely do better than that. What dog? Our dog; and our dog was a wire hair terrier named Dr. Don.

… when a man …

What man? A total stranger? A panhandler asking for money? A CIA agent? Actually, it was none of those. This man owned a hardware store a few blocks away. I might have been in there a couple of times with my father. I remember he looked like all the other store owners. He was short, bald, and weary. He walked over to us, but how did he walk? It was slowly, as if each step was an effort. He wasn't naked (I would have remembered that), so he must have been wearing clothes. I recall they were wrinkled; a wrinkled brown suit and a wrinkled white shirt. I also remember suspenders under his suit jacket.

… stopped us …

If he stopped us, we must have been on our way someplace. Where was it? We were on our way to the bakery to buy bagels. We did that almost every Sunday morning. Now I know where we were walking and why. In fact, I recall we were almost at the bakery.

He recognized my father as a former basketball player.

How do I know he recognized my father? It was the way he came up to us. He was pointing his finger at my father long before he said anything to us. Now I'm ready to rewrite my original pair of sentences into something that paints a better picture.

> My father and I were walking along Kingsbridge Road, past the drug store, on our way to the bakery. Traffic was heavy for a Sunday morning. The old, wheezing buses never took a day off, even though most of the stores that lined the street were closed. Moments from the bakery, a rumpled little man dragged himself over to us. He said nothing at first, but he pointed at my father with an outstretched index finger. Only after two more buses went by did he say, "Did you play basketball?"

Did you see—and I mean that literally—the difference? I suspect you have a good idea of my old neighborhood, the old man, the stores, and the store owners, even if you've never been to the Bronx. How did I do it? How did I transform a generic walk into a snapshot from my life?

I did it with questions.

Starting with those original sentences, which described little more than a location and an event, I asked questions familiar to anyone who ever studied journalism: who, what, when, where, why, and how. WHERE were we walking? WHEN were we walking? WHAT stores lined the street and WHAT one were we walking toward? HOW did I know the man recognized my father?

All these questions jogged my memory and helped me see the details of the scene in my head: the old buses, the traffic, the out-stretched finger. I also recalled details that didn't wind up in the final paragraph. I didn't use the suspenders or wrinkled clothes. But I did combine them into "rumpled," because that's the impression the combination left me with.

Once I saw the details, I decided on the words I would use to help you see what I saw. Were I making a movie, I'd liken what I did to specifying props and costumes. Did I want smoking buses, cough-ing buses, or wheezing buses in my movie? Did I want the store owner wearing wrinkled clothes, rumpled clothes, or sloppy clothes? Like props and costumes, details create a sense of time, place, and mood. They add a sense of reality to your writing and give you tools you can use to create a vivid image for your reader.

Start with your original idea and ask yourself who, what, when, where, why, and how to bring out the details. You'll see what I'm talking about.

You'll see what you're talking about, too.

Post a reply: _____

_____

_____

_____

Production

The film that begins in the mind of a screenwriter takes physical shape during production. The months of pre-production are invisible to the audience. The months of post-production are useless without the actions of the characters and their lines of dialogue all recorded on film. Why, then, in the course of the 2 years it takes to make a typical Hollywood feature are only 40 days devoted to capturing the very essence of the movie on film? The answer sheds light on one of the reasons many writers struggle with their writing.

While the production phase is just another step in the filmmaking process, production has an aura of extraordinary importance because it is the most visible of the three phases. The stars, the scandals, and the overruns are endlessly romanticized in the popular press. Studio tours take civilians through sound stages and back lots—not through pre-production offices.

The production phase is also the first one with easily measurable output. Studio executives may not be able to evaluate the number of storyboards drawn or script lines rewritten, but they can easily count the number of scenes shot per day (and put a dollar value on the results). That kind of measurement makes the phase seem more important, but directors would never complete their films if they didn't attend to all the phases of filmmaking with equal diligence and commitment.

The production phase of the writing process, during which you write your first draft, seems weighty and important, too. Suddenly you have a focus. You have a three-page paper to write, and—look at that—you've written three pages. Life is good. Unlike filmmakers, too many writers place so much emphasis on this phase they don't adequately attend to the other two.

During pre-production, the director's goal is to make the story tangible—to turn it into something actors can act and cinematographers can photograph. During production, the director must guarantee himself and his editor as many choices of performances and camera angles as practical. Which ones he will use is a decision best made by weighing the options in the more reflective climate of post-production.

Rather than thinking about how to write a finished essay, in order, during production, do what filmmakers do. Focus on giving yourself the most choices to work with in post-production. You do that by writing as much about your subject as you can, as fast as you can. Quantity, not quality, is your goal during production. Or, to put it a more memorable way, your goal during production is to produce.

Picture This

A movie is a story told in pictures.

That doesn't mean that essays are relegated to telling their stories exclusively in words. All writing tells a story in pictures. While a director has the advantage of creating images on a 12-foot-tall screen, you have the advantage of creating pictures on a screen as big as your reader's imagination.

Perhaps it makes more sense to say that all writing is visual.

One of the two or three best-kept writing secrets is that the job of a writer is to see a picture in her head and then to write down words that let her reader see the same picture. Screenwriters do this routinely. Through a script, they transfer the film they see in their heads to the director. The director takes the images in her head and turns them into images on the screen. We know what tools the director has at her disposal: actors, cameras, lights, sets, props, and lenses. What do you have?

Words.

Trust me, you have the better deal. Sets, props, equipment, and people cost money. Actors throw snits. Equipment breaks. Scenery doesn't get built on schedule.

Words work for free. They don't talk back. They put in overtime with nary a complaint and are there when you need them—early in the morning, late at night, during lunch, or when you're online.

You do have something in common with a director, though. A director needs the right actors, lighting, sets, props, and equipment. You need the right words to create the right images—the images you see in your head. In subsequent posts, we'll work out the details of telling stories in pictures.

Just like in the movies.

Post a reply: _____

_____

_____

_____

Specific Is Always Better Than General

Write this down: Specific is always better than general. Put it on a card in your wallet, write it on the palm of your hand, or etch it on the inside of your eyelid so you can see it when you close your eyes if you have to. But keep it with you all the time. It's just that important.

Imagine your favorite movie with the stars replaced by ordinary-looking people, people you wouldn't notice if they sat on the bus next to you. While you're at it, replace all the props with cardboard boxes grouped together to suggest furniture, cars, trees, and building lobbies. Oh, and dial back the color so the images are on the border between pale pastels and black and white.

Imagine a film like that and you can imagine your essay when you choose general over specific. Neither one is a pretty picture.

Specific is always better than general.

Of course, there are times when you don't need to describe an event or object in excruciating detail. If you're writing about a walk you took, there's no need to describe every car on the block. If, during the walk, you dash across the street and barely avoid an oncoming vehicle, then tell your reader whether you're escaping from a MINI Cooper or a Mack truck. It makes a difference.

If you're describing a ship sailing to the New World, tell your reader whether the ocean is an inviting blue or a foreboding gray. It makes a difference.

If you're describing how you sing in your church choir every week, tell your reader whether you stand out in the first row or get lost among the robes of the singers in the back. It makes a difference.

Specific is always better than general. It makes a difference you can see.

Post a reply: _____

_____

_____

_____

Rehearsal

Before a director shouts, "Action," he rehearses each scene with his cast and crew. "Rehearsal is incredibly important," says Stephen Hopkins. Hopkins has been directing for over 20 years, and his credits include horror films such as *A Nightmare on Elm Street 5: The Dream Child* and *Predator 2* as well as half the episodes in the first season of *24,* so he knows the value of rehearsing each scene— including the way it relaxes the actors. "Rehearsing allows everyone to understand what the scene is about. Then when you get on the set, you're free to experiment. You can try things this way and that to see if you can make the scene a bit more interesting."

In a way, rehearsing is like brainstorming (see "Brainstorming," page 20). You repeat the same task until the left brain steps out of the way. Then, when you do the job for real, the right brain's creativity, imagination, and playfulness come through.

Before you shoot your first draft, you need some rehearsal time, too. If you were wondering what to do with those index cards from pre-production (see "It's in the Cards," page 36), here's your answer. Grab your cards and head to your rehearsal hall. This should be someplace where you literally put your cards on the table. My students have used large tables in their school libraries, the floors of their living rooms, their dining room tables, and their beds. One of my students used a hotel lobby floor (it was three in the morning and the night clerk appreciated the company).

Lay out your cards in order, just the way you visualized your essay during pre-production. Look at each card and see its main idea in your mind. Remind yourself of all the information you collected.

Refresh your memory about the quotes you pulled from your sources. Spend as much time as you need getting reacquainted with your essay.

Next, neatly pack up all the cards, still in the order in which you'll write your essay, carefully wrap them with a rubber band or two, and put them away.

I mean bury them.

Leave them at the bottom of your underwear drawer, beneath the mattress, or in the back of your closet. Get them out of sight. Forget about them (but don't lose them). It's time to roll the camera.

Write your first draft now, without referencing your index cards. In a way, they're your script, and just as an actor doesn't appear on camera with script in hand, you don't need the cards by your side to write your first draft. That's why you rehearsed.

What you'll discover (and this may surprise you) is that as you work through the draft, the right information will pop into your head as you need it. Actors experience the same sense in their work. Actor Sam Anderson, who counts *Slackers* and *Forrest Gump* among his film credits and whose work in television includes *Lost, NCIS,* and *Grey's Anatomy,* says, "This is something I practice in my work and teach in my acting classes. I do my research and understand what I want to get across in the scene. Then when I get in front of the camera I let go, knowing and trusting that the homework is still there in me and will come out when my fellow actor gives me my cue."

Writers enjoy the same experience. When you sit down to write, you may feel your brain is empty. Once you get your cue, however, the words will flow as if you've known them forever. Here's your cue: I want to tell you a story about _____. Insert the topic of your essay in the blank. If you have some thoughts you want to put down on paper, go ahead. Otherwise, write down the thesis you developed during pre-production. This is it—the moment you've been working toward since you received your assignment. The cast and crew are waiting. Pick up that pencil; boot up that computer; take a confident, measured breath; and shout, "Action."

Hang on. The shooting's started.

Post a reply: _____

_____

_____

_____

State of Mind

Greg Dean is an extraordinarily gifted stand-up comedy teacher. After 30 years of teaching in Los Angeles, Greg counts among his students scores of actors who wanted to perform in comedy clubs or needed to perfect their comedic skills for roles in movies and television.

Dean has many pieces of advice for his students, but one in particular is as important to writers as it is to performers. "Whatever state you're in," Dean tells his students, "that's the state your audience will be in."

No, he doesn't mean if you're in California, so is your audience (although, if you're performing live, there's a lot of good physics behind his words). What Dean means is that if an actor is nervous or angry on stage or in front of the camera, that's the way the audience will feel.

This doesn't mean that an actor can't play a nervous or angry character. Greg is talking about the actor as a real person. If that actor steps into the spotlight nervous and unsure, the audience will be nervous and unsure. If the actor is confident, the audience will be confident, too.

What has this got to do with writing? It turns out that Dean's advice holds true for writers. Whatever state you write your essay in, that's the state your reader will be in. If you are bored when you write your essay, your reader will be bored when she reads it. If you're angry, confused, or downright miserable, that's the state you'll push onto your reader.

As Dean says, "If you don't want to perform in front of an audience that is bored, nervous, or angry, don't walk on stage bored, nervous, or angry. Walk on stage with confidence and a sense of fun and the audience will be right there with you."

What state do you want your teacher to be in when she reads, and possibly grades, your essay? How about that college admissions officer who's reading your personal statement? Then that's the way you want to be when you write. Approach your writing with a sense of confidence and enjoyment and your reader will do the same.

Post a reply: _____

_____

_____

_____

Who Cares?

At the start of production, you'll be poised for takeoff, ready to write, and this voice will come over the intercom in your head.

"This is your left brain speaking. We're just about to depart, but before we do, I have a few announcements. You probably can't write this essay. If you do write it, most likely it won't be any good. If you are turning this essay in for a grade, sit back and relax, because you've already gotten an F. If this is an essay for college, remember that flipping burgers is also a noble profession and one that doesn't require four more years at a school you're not getting into anyway. If you're writing this to enter a contest, you're dumber than I thought. And, remember, if there's anything I can do to make this trip more pleasant, please don't hesitate to ask."

The click of the intercom switching off jolts you back to reality in time to notice a knot in your stomach the size of Philadelphia. At a moment like this there's only one thing to do.

No, don't wrap the intercom cord around the left brain's neck and strangle it to death. Stand up and shake your own hand. Your left brain is putting you through all this because, deep down, it cares about what you're about write. And so do you.

"The difference between hacks and the people who make great stuff is how much you care, how much you're willing to get yelled at, how much you're willing to risk."

Those are the words of writer-director Tom McLoughlin, who began his Hollywood career writing sketch comedy in the 1970s. By the early 1980s he was directing feature films. Since then, his name has been attached, as writer or director, to over 50 film and television projects, giving him ample opportunity to observe the difference interest, passion, and principle make in the quality of a film.

"At the end of the day, if the film doesn't work, what good is having done it? If I compromise or take the easy way out, and if the film's not good, I—and everybody else—look bad," McLoughlin says.

If you don't care about what you write, you won't remember his advice. But I'm betting you will. Because the sweaty palms, the tense shoulders, and the self-doubt all mean that, like McLoughlin, you want to reach the end of the day looking good.

And now you know that's going to happen.

Because you've already decided that you care, that you're willing to take a risk, and that you're willing to get yelled at defending what you believe is the best way to tell the story in your essay.

So flag down the left brain, thank it for its concern, and remind it this is one journey that's going to have a happy landing.

Post a reply: _____

_____

_____

_____

You Talking to Me?

When Robert De Niro uttered "You talkin' to me?" in *Taxi Driver*, it didn't take long for the question to become a classic American catchphrase. But whom, exactly, was De Niro talking to? De Niro's character, Travis Bickle, was talking to himself. But to whom was De Niro the actor talking? The cameraman? The director? His own reflection?

Probably none of these.

De Niro the actor was also talking to Travis Bickle. Robert De Niro, one of the most talented artists in contemporary film, delivered one of the most memorable phrases in contemporary film to a character who was a total figment of his imagination.

This is why De Niro makes the big bucks.

De Niro's business card might say "actor," but his real job is that of communicator. And the best communicators know that all communication takes place between two people. Even when addressing a crowd, good actors perform as if they are talking to only one person. They focus on that woman in the second row or the mustachioed man standing in the corner. Sometimes they do as Bryna Weiss, whom you've seen in films and television roles (including *Gilmore Girls; House, M.D.;* and *Nip/Tuck*) does: they make someone up.

"If I have to talk to a crowd, or if I'm shooting a close-up and just looking into the camera, I talk to my husband, Joe," she says. "Especially when I'm performing on stage in front of an audience. I imagine Joe sitting right in the middle of the theater, and I talk to him."

What's going on? Are actors bred from birth for hallucinogenic qualities? Not at all, according to Weiss. She speaks to her (absent) husband because, as she says, "The person who talks to everyone talks to no one."

That's important enough for me to tell you again:

The person who talks to everyone talks to no one.

What's true in front of an audience is also true behind the keyboard. The writer who writes for everyone truly writes for no one. De Niro has his Bickle, Weiss has her Joe. When you write an essay, whom are you talking to?

When I ask students that question, the most frequent response is a look of surprise. "I'm talking to the person reading my essay," they say (eventually). Sometimes I hear, "I'm talking to a college admissions counselor," or "I'm talking to my teacher." Their surprise grows when I suggest that they follow De Niro and Weiss's leads and talk instead to an imaginary character.

"But wait," you say. "I know who'll read my essay. It's my teacher, a college admissions counselor, or the editor of the school paper." That's a good start. But what do you do when your teacher asks a colleague for a second opinion, your personal essay gets read by two or three admissions counselors, or the editor of the school paper shows your essay to the faculty advisor? Whom are you writing to now?

Just as actors never know who'll see their performances, you don't know who'll read your essays. So address the problem the way actors do and create a mythical reader to write to, then write to that one person alone.

You can choose a friend, a relative, that cute checker at the supermarket, even the teddy bear to whom you entrusted your childhood secrets. Or you can create someone the way De Niro created Bickle. What's important is that you have a clear, detailed picture of this person so you can write your essay as if you were writing or, better yet, talking (see "Let's Talk," page 106) only to him. While you're at it, why not write to someone you'll enjoy sharing your essay with? If you pick someone who wouldn't enjoy your story, what's the fun in telling it to him? Why imagine a stern teacher or a cranky college admissions counselor and let him spoil your fun?

I asked my students how they create ideal readers for their essays. Here are some of their suggestions:

- Create an imaginary reader who will help you write a better essay. If you're concerned your writing gets lost in details, imagine a reader who can't handle complexity and write to him. If you feel your writing tends toward the general, imagine a reader who demands to know all the facts.

- If your essay has some humor in it, pick a reader with a sense of humor. If your essay is sad, pick a reader who won't sob all over the first page until the ink floats away.

- If you feel you're writing to your teacher, decide which teacher you're writing to. Is it the teacher you know from class or the teacher you don't know as a person? Are you writing to your teacher as someone who knows far more about your essay topic than you do or to your teacher as if he were slightly less informed on the subject than you are?

Are you writing to your teacher as someone who wants to hear your story or as someone who is judging you and giving you a grade?

- If you know your essay will be read by a number of people, like a committee of college counselors or the editorial board of a school publication, imagine what qualities all these people share. Admissions counselors are looking for applicants who will bring some interesting points of view to the next freshman class. They're probably looking for a lively essay, because most of what they read is dull and repetitive. They might be tired when they get to your essay, so you need to clear out their cobwebs from the very beginning. Take all these qualities and use them to fashion an imaginary reader, sitting in a dimly lit office, feet on the desk, eyes half closed, wondering if your essay is going to be just like all the others. Now write to that person. Shake him up. Grab his attention. Energize him.

Just the way a reader sees an image of what's in your head (see "Picture This," page 53), a reader can also see an image of whom you're writing to. If so, the reader will become that person, and the essay will seem to be written just for him. That's why it's so important to remember:

The person who speaks to everyone speaks to no one.

If you try to write for everyone, or write to no one, your reader won't know the role he's supposed to play. Like the third person in a two-way conversation, your reader will feel left out, frustrated, and eventually bored.

So if a reader ever asks, "You talkin' to me?" now you can say, politely, "I certainly am." Unless your reader is an angry taxi driver, in which case I suggest taking another cab.

Post a reply: _____

_____

_____

_____

Shoot Out of Order

Imagine a film that opens in the grand ballroom of a luxury hotel. The room is elegantly furnished. At the rear of the room is a wide, sweeping staircase that ascends toward the heavens. While we're at it, let's make it a marble staircase. Even better, let's make it an imported Italian marble staircase. When a filmmaker looks at a set like this, what do you think she sees?

She sees money—lots of money.

There's the money to build the set, the money to strike (disassemble) the set, and the money to rent the studio space during shooting. Now imagine this ballroom appears only at the beginning and end of the film. You can bet the production manager will schedule the filming of the first and last scenes of the movie on consecutive days. Otherwise, the set will have to remain in place, unused, for weeks, collecting dust and rental bills.

That's money—lots of money.

Money is one of the reasons a film's scenes are rarely shot in the order in which they appear on the screen. Another reason is the availability of the actors. Frequently, a well-known actor may appear in half a dozen scenes scattered throughout a movie. The actor, however, only has a few spare days between other commitments. The director will shoot those scenes together, on days she has the actor on the set, no matter where the scenes fall in the story's time line.

Films are shot in an order that works for the filmmaker—an order that maximizes the efficiency of the production. You can borrow this idea and use it to your advantage during your production phase.

We already know what form we expect a movie to take. There's the beginning, where we are introduced to the story; a middle, where the characters battle for what they want; and an end, where we find out whether the hero wins the day.

As audience members, we'd have a hard time with a film that started in the middle, went to the end, then jumped to the beginning just because that's the order in which the film was shot. When the theater lights dim and we stuff our faces full of popcorn, we want to enjoy a well-structured film. We don't know the order in which it was shot. We don't even care.

So it is with the reader of your essay.

Your reader expects to find an essay with the standard structure of introduction, body, and conclusion. She never sees the order in which you wrote your essay, nor does she care. What matters is the version you put up on the big screen, so to speak. Take a moment to appreciate the consequences of this situation. You have incredible freedom to write your essay in an order that's most efficient for you. Like a film, shoot first and put things together later (that's what post-production is for).

Rather than staring at a blank page or computer screen waiting for that perfect first sentence or opening paragraph to pop into your head, write what you do know. You won't be the first writer to work that way.

"When I get stuck on something, I may spend three or four days when I can't get past a scene," says Jeff Wynne. It might be hard to imagine Wynne getting stuck. For 20 years he's earned his living writing movies and animation for television. His income depends upon his ability to deliver scripts on time, so being stuck is not a situation he can indulge.

"I'll skip 20 pages forward and write something that I know I want to write," Wynne says. "I'll get that down just to break the logjam in my head."

So follow Wynne's writing strategy and the working habits of generations of directors. Are you suddenly struck by a support point that's destined to play a starring and compelling role in your essay? Shoot it now, when that star support point is right there, available and fresh in your mind.

Like a filmmaker, your job during production is to capture your story quickly and efficiently. Once you have all the pieces, you will pass them on to the folks in post-production (you, of course) for the final assembly. Right now, go with your internal flow. Write what's hot. Write what wants to come out. You've yelled, "Action," the actors are on their marks, and the cameras are rolling. Your essay is on its way. Enjoy the little surprises you find in your writing. Applaud when you write a cool paragraph. Make your set a fun place to be.

You will look back when your essay is complete and realize this was the second most exciting time of your essay-writing experience.

Post a reply: _____

_____

_____

_____

Hunting for Treasure

Few people want to watch a film in which the hero says, "Well now, I have all the pieces of the treasure map. That's good enough for me. I think I'll take it home and frame it over the fireplace." Maybe in a Woody Allen movie, a Christopher Guest film, or some weird Charlie Kaufman universe, but not in your traditional romp around the world. In a Hollywood blockbuster, the hero never confuses the clues for the treasure. The Hollywood treasure hunter never stops too soon.

Unlike Hollywood heroes, though, writers often do.

In writing, each sentence is a clue to the next sentence, each paragraph a pointer to the one after it. As a writer, your job is to assemble all those clues into a map that points the way to a writer's treasure—that compelling, powerful, can't-stop-reading-until-I-get-to-the-end essay.

Granted, writers don't have directors behind them telling them what the treasure is or what it looks like (though that's partly what this book is for). Writers have to do the job for themselves. Nevertheless, the secret to success, just as in the movies, is not to confuse the clues with the treasure. When writing your production draft, this means recognizing that the first 10, 20, or even 50 percent of what you write may merely be the map that points the way to the guts of your essay. Confusing the map for the treasure means you'll stop too soon.

Your reader will wind up with a map to your essay, but when it comes to understanding the point you want to make, your poor reader won't have a clue.

Post a reply: _____

_____

_____

_____

That All-Important Opening Scene

You've probably had the experience of watching a film's opening scene and knowing almost instantly whether or not this is a ride you're interested in taking.

An essay's opening scene is typically its first paragraph, but arguably the most important part of that paragraph—the place where the essay's hook is set—is the opening sentence. This is why writers seem to put more effort into their opening sentences than any other part of their essay.

Granted, a good opening sentence makes your audience think, "I've got to know what happens next." If you don't want people walking out on your essay right from the start, it seems you have no choice but to polish that opening sentence until you can see your reflection in it.

Just don't do it now.

Trying to find the perfect opening sentence before you've written your essay is a shortcut to disaster, because you don't know what your essay is about. "But wait," you say, "I've done all this research. I've arranged my index cards. I've thought about what I'm going to say for days. I know exactly what I'm writing about."

You do, and you don't.

There's a movie that illustrates this point. It's called *Big*. In the film, Tom Hanks plays Joshua Baskin, a kid who is tired of being a kid. Kids don't have any fun because they're totally under the control of grown-ups. Joshua wants to escape all that. Joshua wants to be big. One morning, thanks to the magical powers of a coin-operated fortune-telling machine, Joshua gets his wish. Joshua wakes up big.

Inside he's the same kid he was yesterday. Outside he looks like a grown-up, and that's the way people act toward him. Suddenly, Joshua discovers what it means to be a grown-up. There are good parts, such as having a romance with a woman and becoming a successful toy company marketing executive, and there are bad parts, such as the responsibilities that come with adulthood and the sudden distance he has from his friends, who don't want to play with an adult.

Had someone told Joshua that growing up too soon was highly overrated, he no doubt would have pooh-poohed the idea up one side of the Brooklyn Bridge and down the other. Having discovered what being big was all about on his own, Joshua had a much better idea about who he was and who he wanted to be.

You are Joshua (in a manner of speaking, of course) before you become big. You see the world in front of you, your essay, from one perspective. You can't know what other perspectives there are until you discover them. Joshua had magic on his side. You have your writing.

As you work through production and post-production, your essay will grow up and you'll make connections and discover ideas, opinions, and thoughts about your topic that are impossible for you to predict right now—as impossible as it was for young Joshua to predict what life would be like when he was big. Since your opening sentence introduces your grown-up essay— and since, like Joshua, you don't know quite what that's like right now—you can see that slaving away on an opening sentence, or searching for the perfect one, is not a good idea. Most professional writers will tell you that the number of times the opening sentence on the first draft was the same opening sentence on the final draft could be counted on the fingers of one hand after they cut most of them off.

And these are professionals—men and women who make their livings writing articles, stories, screenplays, and novels. If they can't predict what their grown-up writing will be like, it's doubtful you can, either.

So be kind to yourself. Write down whatever opening sentence you need to get started (see "Shoot Out of Order," page 69). You'll find your real opening sentence as your writing gets big during post-production.

Where you find that sentence will be one of the biggest surprises of your writing process.

Post a reply: _____

_____

_____

_____

One Scene, Many Takes

Steven Spielberg makes a movie. The movie is 2 hours and 20 minutes long. When it's over, 12,600 feet of film has run through the projector. To get those 12,600 feet, Spielberg had to shoot 126,000 feet of film. That's nearly 24 miles of film, only a couple of miles shy of a marathon.

Steven Spielberg needs to run a marathon to make a film? He seemed like such a sharp guy. What's going on?

Directors shoot far more film than ever winds up in the finished movie because they shoot multiple takes and coverage (see "Coverage," page 79). This post is about those multiple takes.

You probably know what they are. Multiple takes are immortalized in films, television shows, and commercials. There's that hand holding the chalkboard with the moveable bar on top (the contraption is called the "sticks"). Written on the sticks are the words "Scene" and "Take." An off-screen voice shouts, "Scene one, take two." There's a loud snap, the director yells, "Action," and something wonderful happens. Multiple takes—refilming the same scene with the same actors, actions, and dialogue—capture different versions of the same performance. These takes offer directors and editors choices during post-production, and these choices are best made away from the pressure and clamor of the set.

When your essay gets to post-production, you'll want choices, too. Create those choices now, the way filmmakers do. When you finish a paragraph (or a sentence) and feel you could write it another way, do so. Start your next take right where you are. Even though writing the same paragraph in different ways may feel like a waste of time, you'll appreciate having the choices during post-production.

How might your takes vary from one to the other?

You might phrase the same thought differently, use a different analogy or metaphor, or restructure the paragraph. Turn it upside down, beginning it at the end, or recast some of the sentences, playing around with the ratio of simple to complex ones. You might start with the same idea and see if you can reach different conclusions.

If you write your first draft in longhand, try drawing lines or brackets in the margin to remind yourself that groups of paragraphs are multiple takes. When you glance over the draft, those markings will give you a quick read on how many takes you're working with. If you're using a computer, try using different fonts for different takes or put your alternate takes in italics.

Not every paragraph is a candidate for multiple takes. If you reach the end of a paragraph and no variations come to mind, call it a wrap and move on.

Like a Hollywood star, you might get it right the first time, too.

Post a reply: _____

_____

_____

_____

Coverage

Here's the scene: We see a living room, a generously overstuffed living room, with floor-to-ceiling windows overlooking a patio and swimming pool. The room is filled with high school–age boys and girls. They're clumped into groups of two, three, and four. Beer cans fill the spaces between the groups.

Suddenly, we hear a car pull into the driveway.

Everyone freezes. There's a cut to the sofa where the sound has interrupted a rather deep embrace. Let's skip some questionable lines of clichéd dialogue and say that, as the couple on the sofa discusses the potential consequences of the premature arrival of her parents, the image on the screen switches to a close-up of him, a close-up of her, him, her, a shot of the two of them together, and finally a shot of the whole room as the partygoers scatter like cockroaches in the light.

Get the picture?

Now let's see how the director got that picture onto the screen. First, he shot the whole scene with a wide view that included the room and everyone in it. Then he moved the camera in and shot the couple on the sofa as a medium shot, with both of them on the screen. Then he moved the camera again, this time to a close-up of the boy as he recited only his lines. One more move and the director shot the girl in close-up as she delivered her dialogue.

That's one scene shot from four different perspectives.

Those different perspectives provided what filmmakers call coverage. Coverage differs from multiple takes because, with multiple takes, the director doesn't move the camera. The goal is to find the right performance from a single perspective. When shooting coverage, the director looks at a single performance from different points of view.

You can use the principle of coverage when you write your essays. Think of your coverage as writing as many essay support points as you can wring from your pre-production research. Imagine that each support point is a different perspective on why your thesis is valid. Like shooting multiple takes of the same scene (see "One Scene, Many Takes," page 77), coverage gives you choices during post-production.

What kinds of choices?

Certainly you'll want to consider your best performances—those supporting paragraphs you feel are the strongest. But you may also find two support points of equal strength. Now you can choose the one that best fits into the flow of your essay.

Coverage also serves as an insurance policy against a disaster. Sooner or later, you'll have to throw away one of your favorite support points because it's wrong. Suppose you copy down a quote incorrectly or you're so sure you know what you're writing about that you don't double-check your facts only to discover, much later, that you have a major hole right in the middle of your argument. The writing gods like to have their fun with us every now and then. You might not be thrilled with your lack of thoroughness, but at least you caught the error before turning in your assignment. Meanwhile, if you have enough coverage, you can always salvage your work.

Like multiple takes, coverage may feel like a waste of time. After all, why do more writing than you need to do? Here's why: when you do 110 percent of what you need to do and you achieve your goal, you've wasted 10 percent of your effort. If you do 90 percent of what you need to do and don't achieve your goal, you've wasted 90 percent of your effort.

A little coverage pays 110 percent dividends.

Post a reply: _____

_____

_____

_____

Actions Speak Louder Than Words (Even Though We Need the Words to Describe the Actions)

There's nothing that captures the attention of an audience like a good, old-fashioned love scene. Let's create one. We'll put a couple in a romantic restaurant setting, with wine, candles, and soft music. We'll shoot two versions. In the first one, the man gently caresses the woman's hand, gazes softly into her eyes, and quietly says, "I love you."

Here's version two. The man looks past his companion, as if a patch of wallpaper behind her were far more important than she is. "I love you," he says.

In which version do you believe the man loves the woman? It's almost nonsensical to ask, isn't it? But wait. Why do you believe the man in the first version and not the second? After all, he did profess his love both times in plain, straightforward English.

Blame your belief or disbelief on what he did, not what he said. In the second scene, his staring into the distance undercuts his words, while his actions in the first scene reinforce what he says. People are how they act, not what they say.

We want the characters in films to take actions because we need to see people in action to understand who they are and what they want. How does that work in your production draft? It's easy to slip into paragraphs of descriptions about people—what they're wearing, where they're standing, what they're seeing, what they're feeling. It's harder, but more effective, to describe their actions and the choices they're making that tell your reader all she needs to know about their character, personality, and emotional condition.

Your father may be kind and considerate. You could dip into the thesaurus and find two dozen words to describe his kindness and consideration. Or you could tell us that, one day, the two of you were out for a walk when you saw a child drop her ice cream cone. As she started to cry, your father walked over to a nearby snack stand and bought this little stranger a new ice cream cone.

Actions not only speak louder than words, they also speak directly to your reader. Describing your father as "kind and considerate" rules out his being "extremely kind and considerate," "uniquely kind and considerate," or "compulsively kind and considerate." When measuring your father's character by his actions, your reader will put him in the category that means the most to her.

I often use this example in my workshops, and then I ask the students, "What kind of a man do you think that father was?" One day a student piped up, "I wish he were my father." Another said, "I wish I were the little girl." Everybody laughed.

Try to evoke that reaction with a string of adjectives.

Post a reply: _____

_____

_____

_____

The 15-Minute Rule

The hardest part of the essay-writing process might be putting words on paper. There are a dozen reasons why, and discussing any or all of them won't make any difference in the way you, or just about any other writer, works. Sit down to put words on paper and suddenly you discover 3,000 incredibly important tasks you could or should deal with at that moment.

Let me propose this little movie and see if it resonates with you. By and large, the setting is inside my brain, so you might want to imagine this as an animated movie. The alternatives get a little weird, not to mention gory. This is what seems to play out in my head when I sit down, pick up my pencil, and stare at the infamous blank page.

EYES: Hello, Brain? He's looking at his pencil.

RIGHT HAND: Oh, noooo, Brain. We know what that means. Doooo something.

BRAIN: Memory Bank Three, this is Mission Control. Talk to me.

MB3: Roger, Mission Control. I have plants not watered in two days. I have three pictures that need straightening. The computer desktop needs to be cleaned up.

BRAIN: That's it?

MB3: And we're low on ice cubes.

BRAIN: Roger that. Adrenal glands, this is Mission Control. Condition Red. I repeat, Condition Red.

A quick cut to the adrenal glands atop the kidneys. They glow blue, then yellow, then orange, then bright orange. A purple streak zaps from the glands and powers its way north.

EYES: Oh, noooo, we're growing bigggger.

Cut to my face as my eyes grow wide, my eyebrows arch, and my expression turns blank. My right hand, which had been reaching for my pencil, comes to a dead halt somewhere in midair. Like a man possessed, possessed of an upset stomach and desperately in need of a bathroom, I leap from my chair. Cut to the kitchen, where I fling open the freezer door with my right hand. In my left hand is the recipe for ice.

All writers, it seems, have an infinite capacity for delaying the putting of words on paper. After way too many years and far too much ice-making, I discovered what I call the 15-Minute Rule. The underlying theory is I can stand anything for 15 minutes. When I have a writing project, I work on it for 15 minutes and no more.

BRAIN: All right, listen up. We're going to put some words on paper for 15 minutes.

RIGHT HAND: Oh, noooo.

BRAIN: It's just 15 lousy minutes.

MB3: That's what you said yesterday, and didn't we work for …?

Suddenly, the communications channel goes dead.

BRAIN: Now, where were we?

ALL SYSTEMS: Oh, noooo.

That's the deal. I will write for 15 minutes, and at the end of that time, I will stand up, make ice, clean up my computer desktop, straighten the pictures, text my friend Jack, oil the can opener, and replace my sneaker laces. But first, I'm going to write for 15 minutes.

And that's exactly what I do, followed, usually, by an hour and a half more.

If there's one thing I want you to remember from this post, and this book, it is that all writers have brains that work overtime finding reasons not to put words on paper—until we start.

Then, like the need to make ice, everything else melts away.

Post a reply: _____

_____

_____

_____

Backstory

Here's something you probably never think about: what were your favorite film characters doing before the start of their movies?

I'm not referring to where Brad and Angelina were hanging out or what summer job Katie had when she was 16. I mean, what were the CHARACTERS those stars played doing in the days or weeks before their films started? Or in the case of Indiana Jones, what was he doing in the 19 years between his last two films?

Screenwriters and filmmakers call this life before the backstory—the details of a character's life before the action of a film begins. Sometimes, a film lets you in on the backstory. A flashback is the most direct way because it shows you exactly what happened days, weeks, or years ago.

Other ways of revealing the backstory are slightly less direct, like when characters talk about what happened to them in off-screen incidents. At other times the reveal is more subtle because the backstory is suggested by a character's seemingly out-of-character behavior. The aforementioned Indiana Jones, a swashbuckling hero in all other respects, is deathly afraid of snakes. We all know something happened, and whatever it was involved a snake, but we don't know the details. The mysterious incident is part of Jones's backstory. The specifics may be revealed someday, but for now they're left to our imaginations.

Indy's past, his backstory, affects the present. If Indy encounters snakes, the story is about to take an unpredictable turn because we, the audience, and the characters in the story can no longer count on Indy to be a no-holds-barred hero, charging ahead with abandon.

The next time you watch a film, see how much of the backstory you can glean from the characters and storyline. Pay attention to how much more you know about the story going forward when you have an idea about the story looking backward.

During production, keep in mind that the backstory of your essay often deepens and strengthens your argument. For example, suppose you are writing an essay on labor unions in mid-twentieth-century America. Your support includes statistics on wages, hours worked, employee benefits, the rise of leisure time, the use of child labor, home ownership, and population shifts from rural to urban to suburban locales.

What constitutes a backstory for this topic? Try looking at life before unions. How did workers spend their days (and nights)? Who were the people behind the rise of unions? What motivated them to take on a cause shunned by others?

Chances are, you came across this information during your research and it's buried somewhere in your deck of index cards (see "It's in the Cards," page 36). As you start writing your first draft, that information might be knocking on the door, asking to be included in your writing. By all means, invite it in.

Maybe you're thinking that the backstory is not what the teacher asked for. Perhaps she's a stickler for the nuts and bolts of the topic. That's fine. Invite the backstory in anyway. As in films, the backstory in your essay might never appear directly. Instead, it may underlie your story, provide some context without drawing attention to itself. Either way, the production phase is not the time to make this decision. But the backstory cannot enhance your essay if you don't know what the backstory is.

You can prove this to yourself.

Let's suppose that, in 1952, the average union worker's wage was 20 percent higher than his nonunion counterpart. Write a short paragraph using that fact as a support point for this thesis: Without unions, the mid-twentieth-century worker would have been enslaved by his employer. Write a support point now.

Let's combine that 20 percent figure with some backstory. Unions didn't simply happen. Some of the efforts to unionize industries were marked by riots, violence, and loss of life. Rewrite your supporting paragraph and incorporate this bit of the backstory. Write that second paragraph now.

Chances are good that your second paragraph is not only more interesting, it's more compelling. What once was a paragraph that stated some facts has developed some human interest. Union workers enjoyed wage gains, but those extra dollars came at an even greater cost when measured in terms of human life. This bit of backstory transforms the meaning of the word "better" from "better" equals "improved" to "better" equals "improved, but at great cost."

The ability to put support in context is the power of backstory. Write the backstory as you write your production draft. We'll explore that power in post-production.

Post a reply: _____

_____

_____

_____

Too Much Is Never Enough

This is a short post, but an important one, so it's getting a space of its own.

Most screenwriters write first drafts of their screenplays that run 160, 180, even 200 pages. Some write more. Their finished scripts run about 100 to 120 pages. What screenwriters know is an important lesson to carry over into your own writing: it's easier to find 120 good pages in 200 than it is to find 120 good pages in 100.

During production, you're going to do what screenwriters do. You're going to overproduce. Plan on writing 1½ to 2 times the number of pages called for in the assignment. It's easier to find 5 good pages in 10 than 5 good pages in 3.

Write that down someplace where you will see it every day during production. It's easier to find 5 good pages in 10 than 5 good pages in 3. You can thank me later.

Post a reply: _____

_____

_____

_____

Add Conflict

Your brother or sister (cast that role for yourself) walks into the room and grabs your most prized possession. You know what it is.

"I want this," he/she says.

"Okay," you say absentmindedly, as you read your text messages.

Your sibling was expecting a full-scale battle, but you didn't take the bait. Instead, your room is filled with a sense of peace, harmony, and downright normalcy.

Rather a dull story, isn't it?

"There's an old Hollywood saying that drama is life with all the boring parts cut out," says Jeffrey Davis, chair of the screenwriting program at Loyola Marymount University in Los Angeles. Davis began his career as a sitcom writer and now writes plays in addition to teaching future screenwriters their craft. According to Davis, getting rid of the boring parts means throwing in a hearty helping of conflict.

"I can't watch a nature documentary," says Davis, "unless the lion is eating something."

Peace, harmony, and normalcy may be desirable states of affairs in the real world, but in movies what the audience thirsts for is conflict. Filmmakers are only too happy to oblige. Watch a movie carefully and you'll see conflict in the arc of the story—the journey from beginning to end—along with small doses of conflict in just about every scene. The idea of two people wanting something that only one of them can have is the engine that propels the film's story forward.

Conflict doesn't always mean a fight. Conflict occurs when two people see different sides of the same issue. She sees marriage as a wonderful gift. He sees marriage as a prison. She wants to go to a small college in Oregon. Her parents are booking the hotel they will stay at during her graduation from Columbia.

Small differences can generate emotional energy that keeps the story moving, and that energy is contagious. Yes, the conflict is in the film, but it quickly spreads to the audience—to you. That's one way a well-made film makes you feel like part of the action.

Conflict in your essay is contagious, too. You create conflict by making sure you include both sides of the argument surrounding your thesis.

"But wait," you say, "didn't you insist that a good thesis argues only one side of an issue?" Absolutely true (see "The First 10 Minutes," page 12). The thesis should argue for only one side. That doesn't mean your essay can't air opposing points of view and demonstrate why, in your opinion, those views lack substance.

Although it may seem a little self-defeating, raising the opposing argument in your own essay is a wise strategy. Maybe we watch too many films or television shows. Maybe it's the way our brains work. Whether it's the adrenaline rush that comes from conflict or simply curiosity about what's around the corner, conflict—like a flickering fire—is difficult to ignore. If conflict doesn't exist, we generate it. (After all, why did your sibling want your most PRIZED possession?) You can pretty much bet that, from the start, your readers are thinking about counterexamples to your support points.

Since your reader already has conflict on her mind, make that work for you by balancing your argument with opposing arguments. We'll work out the details during post-production, but during production, focus on getting that conflict down on paper. As you write a support point, take a beat and write the paragraph you might write if you were arguing the opposite point of view.

One way to uncover this sort of conflict is by imagining you are in a conversation with someone who's arguing the opposite side of the issue (see "Some Days You're Not Yourself," page 94).

By addressing both sides of your thesis, you'll satisfy your reader's need for conflict. And when she's done reading, she won't have anything to argue about.

Post a reply: _____

_____

_____

_____

Some Days You're Not Yourself

Ever have a day when you didn't feel like yourself? Terrific. That's all the experience you need to add some zest to your writing.

In a previous post (see "Add Conflict," page 91) I hinted at a way of finding the conflict in your essay by pretending to be in a conversation with someone who's arguing against your thesis. No more hints. Here's a step-by-step guide.

Change hats for a moment and, instead of writing an essay, pretend you're writing a screenplay. Imagine a scene between you and another person, the not you—the person who's not yourself. The two of you are seated … well, where are you? Are you in your kitchen, the library, a bus? See the location in your mind. See the two of you there. You are arguing the thesis that there is no such thing as luck, that people who seem lucky are really people who have prepared themselves for opportunity. Start the conversation between you and your imaginary opponent. Your job is to record it as if you were a court stenographer.

> **YOU:** Luck isn't random. People are lucky because they are prepared.
>
> **NOT YOU:** Nonsense. There are things beyond our control. There's truth to the saying, "Being in the right place at the right time."
>
> **YOU:** <Your first support point goes in here.>
>
> **NOT YOU:** <The counterargument to this first point goes in here.>

YOU: <Argue against this counterargument. Offer a point of your own in here.>

NOT YOU: <Refute this new point with another point of your own here.>

Keep at it until you have the makings of some good conflict. Now you can return to (or start) your production draft. Work the conflict in when it feels comfortable. Not every point you raise needs to be, nor deserves to be, countered by your imaginary opponent. Remember our rule, at least during production: when in doubt, write it down.

Pick a literary fight and see how it keeps your essay moving forward.

Post a reply: _____

_____

_____

_____

Dreadful Drafts

One of these days, you may discover you can't write. This doesn't mean that, like Joel Barish in *Eternal Sunshine of the Spotless Mind,* you've had your brain wiped and, in your case, something went way wrong and you no longer remember your spelling, grammar, and punctuation. You can't write because you're not able to put words down on paper. Nearly every writer's been there, and they know that feeling is one of the most frustrating, debilitating, and downright freaky feelings in the world.

When the words aren't coming, it's often because the left brain won't give up control of the writing process. You've tried brain-storming (see "Brainstorming," page 20), taking a nap, putting the work aside for a while, and working on other projects; but when you return to whatever has you stymied, whoops, there's the left brain, arms crossed, tapping its foot, waiting for you. Apparently, the left brain didn't get the memo that, during production, any-thing goes. It is waiting for you to write what it considers a good essay. So far, it's not impressed. Instead, it thinks all you're capable of is junk.

Fine. If that's what your left brain thinks, prove it right. Take an hour to write a dreadful draft of your essay. (This does not mean a draft that's unintelligible because it demolishes the rules of spelling and grammar. You need to be able to read it to judge it dreadful, after all.) If you're wondering how dreadful, here's a guideline. Imagine you will be sending me your draft. If I'm able to find a paragraph—no, a sentence; no, not even a sentence, a phrase—that forms the nucleus of an idea for a good essay, I get your entire music collection. All your CDs, everything in your com-puter, and all the tracks on your iPod become mine, mine, mine. I don't mean COPIES of all your music, I mean ALL YOUR MUSIC. Oh, and I want your iTunes user name and password so you can't get any of it back. (Okay, you're not actually going to send me your essay, but in the spirit of the movies, pretend you are.)

Before you start writing, though, I have to warn you: I've shared this activity with hundreds of students and if I wanted to, I could have the largest music collection in the known world. To date, not one of my students was able to write a perfectly dreadful draft. I haven't researched the subject, but from my experience I'm inclined to believe it can't be done. When you read your dreadful draft, you'll find yourself thinking, "That's not so bad," "I like that," or "That could work."

Once you know you can't write a perfectly dreadful draft, your somewhat embarrassed left brain will ease off and you'll be free to write your production draft.

Post a reply: _____

_____

_____

_____

Put a Face on It

Have you ever seen a film about a thing? You probably haven't and probably never will. Feature films are all about people. Through animation, films can tell stories about animals and objects, but the animals and objects behave as if they were people. Even documentaries, which may bear lofty titles such as *Victory at Sea; Food, Inc.;* or *Berkeley in the Sixties,* are not about the sea, food, or Berkeley in the sixties. These films are about the people involved with World War II, the big business of feeding America, or ground zero of the Free Speech Movement.

Writing about people gives you the opportunity to tell a dynamic story. Writing about things gives you the opportunity to write a description. (Want some proof? Read an instruction manual. That's the ultimate writing about a thing.)

When an essay assignment calls for you to write about a thing—a book; a historical event; an abstract concept such as love, luck, or truth—explore ways to adjust your thesis to write about the people involved.

Writers call this "putting a face on it."

When you put a face on something, you tell your story through the eyes of another person (or yourself if you are writing a personal essay). Here's an example you can try right now.

One complaint about furniture, a complaint that endures across generations, is that newer furniture is never as well made, sturdy, durable, long-lasting, comfortable, quiet, or fresh-smelling as the furniture of a generation ago. What do you think? Pick a piece of furniture in your room, apartment, house, or doctor's waiting room. Do you think it's as well made as its ancestors? There's your thesis: yes it is or no it's not.

First, write a short essay—no more than a page—supporting your thesis. The essay doesn't have to be perfect. Just focus on the furniture. Describe what it looks like; how it's made; what's good or bad about its shape, construction, or design. Keep people out of your story. Hammer it out the way you might a first draft. In fact, put a time limit on yourself of 15 to 20 minutes. Write your page and then read on.

Put your essay aside and write another one using the same thesis. This time, argue your thesis by writing about some incident, situation, or story involving you (or some other person) and the piece of furniture. Maybe you fell asleep in a chair and woke up with aches in places you never knew existed. Perhaps a creaky bed kept your cousin up all night before a big exam or the new sofa in your living room doesn't collect as much loose change as the sofa you grew up with. Write this one-page essay now.

This next part is easy. Put both essays down for a day. Browse other posts in this book, but come back here tomorrow and we'll take a look at what you wrote.

If it's tomorrow (honestly, you have to let your work sit for a day because it will make a difference), reread both essays starting with the first one—the one that concentrates on the piece of furniture. When you've read both of them, jot down the differences between the two from the perspective of a reader rather than a writer.

Which essay had more emotion? Which essay told a more interesting story? Which essay practically begged you to keep reading? Which essay felt more human? Which essay could you, as a reader, identify with?

Yes, you might have guessed at the answers without writing the essays, but we learn about writing by experiencing it, and now you've experienced the differences for yourself. Putting a face on it dramatically improves the tone, feel, and appeal of an essay when the topic is a thing or concept.

When you brainstorm your thesis (see "Brainstorming," page 20) and your first draft (see "It's in the Cards," page 36), do some brainstorming about the people involved in your topic and how you might write your essay from their point of view or with their kind of insight.

Putting a face on your topic will give your essay a whole new look.

Post a reply: _____

_____

_____

_____

Make the Story Yours

Sometime during production you're going to wonder if what you're writing is all that unique. You'll imagine that your reader has read it so many times that, on his deathbed, his final words will be your story, line for line. When that happens, rent and study the films *Romeo and Juliet, West Side Story,* and *Twilight.* These are three widely different movies: an Elizabethan love story, a battle between rival New York City gangs, and a tale of temptation and desire as vampires cross paths with the living. You might be hard pressed to find three more disparate films. Disparate, that is, except for one tiny detail.

They are all the same story.

Strip away the costumes and the settings, the character names and the dialogue, and what's left is a story about two star-crossed lovers whose families (literal or symbolic) are determined to keep them apart.

So who sues whom for plagiarism?

The answer is nobody—not even Shakespeare, whose work predates the others. Chances are, even the Bard found his inspiration in someone else's writing. Identical stories are alive and well, some writers claim, because there are only so many different story types (though the range varies from 36 to 32,768, depending on who you ask). At this point in human evolution, so the thinking goes, it's impossible to find a story that's never been told.

Nevertheless, there are few successful plagiarism suits between filmmakers. This is not because filmmakers are all ladies and gentlemen but because all films tell their stories in unique ways. While a screenwriter and director may begin with two lovers ripped apart by society, the details, characters, and events all team up to make a film unique even when the underlying story is familiar.

"But wait," you say, "haven't I heard this before? Didn't you write a post about details?" Yes (see "I've Got a Question," page 46). Details bring your writing alive. Details create those all-important images in your reader's mind (see "Picture This," page 53). Now you know something else about details: details make your writing yours.

There are probably a million people on Earth (a safe guess with three billion or so of us) who could write an essay in which they were walking with their father and family dog when they were stopped by someone on the street (see "I've Got a Question," page 46). There's only one essay like mine, with my father and my dog, along with the wheezing buses, the stores on Kingsbridge Road, a rumpled man, and an outstretched finger.

Just as there's only one essay like yours.

Post a reply: _____

_____

_____

_____

Implements of Construction

The number one question I'm asked at workshops or speaking engagements is "What's the best way to start an essay?" Take a guess at what the number two question is.

It's "What do you write with?"

Many nonwriters seem to believe that mimicry, in the form of a preoccupation with writing utensils, is some shortcut to fame and fortune—if I write the way a successful author does, I will be successful. Writers know better.

Certainly what you write with affects how well you write, in the sense of whether your hand grows tired or your writing becomes illegible. Less well known is that what you write with affects how well you write psychologically. Understanding your writing process includes discovering what you enjoy writing with and when you enjoy writing with it. Nothing, not even the perfect writing instrument, lasts forever (although adolescence seems like it does), and what you want to write with at noon may change by tea time.

One way to understand what works for you, of course, is through experimentation. Here are some discoveries made by my students over the years. You might use their experiences as your starting point:

- First drafts are best written in longhand and in pencil. A mechanical pencil is good for writing anywhere, though the Mirado Black Beauty pencil is popular if you can carry a pencil sharpener with you.

- Writing longhand gives you more of a connection between the words in your head and the way they appear on paper. When you emphasize a word in your head you may notice it comes out a little bigger or a little darker on paper. You can't do that with a computer.

- Writing production drafts on a computer hampers creativity because the words look so good, so final, you often feel hesitant to change them.

- Rewrite on a computer because cut and paste trumps finality.

- Write first drafts in spiral-bound notebooks rather than on yellow pads. You are less likely to lose pages that way.

- Cross out rather than erase.

- Write .txt files and not .doc or .docx files on the computer so you don't get hung up on fonts, margins, underlining, and the like.

Now it's your turn. What do you like about the writing tools you use? What don't you like? What other writing tools can you use? Try them and see what difference, positive or negative, they make in your writing process. Experiment with different ones during pre-production, production, and post-production. One of my students uses a Sharpie pen to write on her index cards, a pencil and paper for her production drafts, and a laptop computer during post-production.

Another student put it this way: "When I don't have my favorite tools I can still write, but I'm tentative and slightly disoriented— the way I feel when using a friend's bathroom."

Now's the time to find your own comfortable writing tools and, hopefully, a more comfortable analogy.

Post a reply: _____

_____

_____

_____

Let's Talk

Sometimes during production you're going to get stuck. You'll feel like the words are right there, someplace, but for some reason they can't find their way to the page.

That's when it's time to have a good long talk with yourself. Well, not exactly yourself. It's time to talk to an imaginary reader (see "You Talking to Me?," page 64).

I learned this trick from one of my students. She wrote by imagining she was a stenographer and her job was to transcribe a conversation between two people—herself as a writer, and a skeptical imaginary reader, Heloise.

My student would write a sentence and then she'd imagine what Heloise would say in response. For example, she might write "Our country would be better off if we switched to ethanol."

"Better off in what way?" Heloise would say.

"Better off because we would reduce our dependence on foreign oil, make use of crops we might otherwise throw away, and build factories that would employ people and put money into the economy," my student would say. Then she'd slip into her role of stenographer and write it all down.

"Says you," Heloise would say. "We could feed those crops to cattle and use the meat to feed starving people." Or "It's going to take money to build factories. And we'll take away people's land, where they've lived for years." Heloise was clearly on a roll.

My student patiently answered every one of Heloise's questions. If she didn't know the answer, she'd excuse the stenographer; retire to her computer, her books, or the library; and find out. Then she'd sit down with Heloise, call in the stenographer, and start the conversation again.

Then my student read over the transcript of the conversation, edited out Heloise's questions (and her occasional snide comments), and found herself with a pretty good production draft.

There are many ways to keep the words flowing during production, and if having a conversation with an imaginary reader is an idea that works for you, talk it up.

Post a reply: _____

_____

_____

_____

Help, I'm Stuck

If you're like most writers, sometime during production or post-production you're going to feel stuck. When you do, remember that feeling stuck happens. It's a normal part of the writing process. After 50-plus years in the business, screenwriter and playwright Shirl Hendryx says, "I'm stuck so often I'm surprised when I'm not stuck."

When you're working on an essay—an essay that drags along with it the baggage of a deadline and a grade—feeling stuck can also feel life-threatening (or career- or no-more-texting-privileges-threatening). That's normal, too. None of the conscientious writers or students I know want to miss a deadline, even if it means staying up all night and walking around the next day with bloodshot eyes striped like an American flag. The danger of feeling stuck is that when you do, more stuck happens.

Back in the 1960s, there was a novelty toy that was a popular prize at fairs and carnivals. The toy was a woven straw tube about 6 inches long and slightly bigger around than a chubby thumb. After putting your index fingers in opposite sides of the tube, the idea was to remove your fingers. The catch was that the harder you pulled your fingers outward, the tighter the tube gripped them. The normal, obvious, intuitive process of getting unstuck ensnared you even more. The way to free yourself from the toy's grip was to not try at all. If, instead of pulling out, you pushed your fingers in, the tube relaxed and you could gently remove your fingers one at a time. So it is with writing. Rather than fighting to get unstuck, accept that you're stuck and relax.

When you feel stuck, the first thing you can do is stop working on your writing project. Yes, with a deadline looming, not working sounds like the worst possible solution. Of course, so does pushing your fingers further into a straw toy.

Put your work aside and do something mindless. Try exercising, taking a shower, or reading a book for pleasure (a nice novel or a nonfiction book on a topic you're interested in). Most of the time, the solution to whatever has you feeling stuck will pop into your head and you can return to your writing.

Another trick you can use is lowering your expectations. One of the worst things you can do to yourself is set a hard limit on the number of pages you're going to write per day or per hour. The authors of many writing books claim that setting minimums is the secret of success. All too often, though, you'll find yourself concentrating on the words as if they were points in a basketball game. Two words here, three words there, all hard fought, all thoroughly devoid of fun. Instead of immersing yourself in the pleasures of storytelling, you're barreling up and down the court getting shoved, bumped, and thoroughly exhausted in the process.

When you feel stuck, ask yourself what your expectations are. Are they working out? If not, what reasonable expectations can you set? What can you handle at that moment? Give yourself permission to recalibrate your expectations, then move ahead. The 15-minute rule (see "The 15-Minute Rule," page 84) is one implementation of this principle in which you set low expectations from the start.

Another trick is being sensitive to your personal productivity pattern. Here's how one student describes his productivity: "I can write nonstop for about two hours. If I push on, I write sporadically during the next hour. By the fourth hour, if I haven't taken a break, I might get 10 or 15 minutes' worth of useful output. I have two options. I can write for four solid hours, understanding that my last two hours will, on average, be less than half as productive as my first two, or I can write for two hours, take a break, and write for a few more hours. That way, I will produce four hours' worth of output in five or six hours rather than less than three hours' worth of output in four."

What he can't do is demand that hours three and four be as productive as hours one and two. Perhaps, in extraordinary situations, he can hit that stride. But that's not his normal writing process. He can't depend on four hours in four hours all the time, and he tampers with his process at his own peril.

When you're feeling stuck, ask yourself where you are in your daily writing process. Are you pushing the bounds? Are you attempting to change your process in real time? Is that necessary? Are you mistaking a feeling of being stuck for nothing more than the normal rhythms of your writing process? Is it time to take a break?

Yet another trick used by one of my students is writing opening sentences. "But wait," you say, "didn't you write a whole post about not spending time during production on the opening sentence?" Yes, I did (see "The First 10 Minutes," page 12). That post deals with real opening sentences, the ones that will grace the start of your finished essay. My student is talking about pretend opening sentences.

"When I feel stuck, I write serious opening sentences, silly opening sentences, sentences in rhyme, anything I can think of to jiggle my thoughts around. After a while, something clicks. I'll have a couple of ideas in the same sentence and I'll see they're related in a way I never thought of. A silly opening sentence will suddenly make sense if I move a few words around or substitute a more substantial word for a frivolous one. I'm back in the flow of writing, and I pick up a potentially useful opening sentence in the process."

One of the causes of that sinking, stuck feeling is having too many compelling thoughts. Opening sentences, in general, serve to focus the essence of an essay into a dozen words or so. A pretend opening sentence can answer the question "What's my most important thought?" for you.

A final trick to try when feeling stuck is changing your writing location. A perceptive former screenwriting student of mine noticed this. "I write very well in four places: my office, hotel rooms, libraries, and coffee shops. I write somewhat well in my kitchen and in my bathroom. I cannot write at all in my bedroom, on airplanes, inside a moving car, or in front of people I know."

Knowing where you write well—and where you don't—is part of knowing your writing process. One question to ask yourself when you're feeling stuck is whether you are in one of your preferred writing locations. If not, move if you can. If you're in one of your preferred places, move to another one. Are there people around you while you're writing? Move to a quiet place for a while. Are you writing in your room and you're noticing that the paint on the wall is beginning to talk to you? It's time to find a busy location that's on your preferred list. You may not believe this until you try it, but changing locations will change your whole attitude about your writing assignment.

Writing locations also burn out. A location that rocked for months can suddenly feel cold and confining. When that happens, give the location a rest and allow it to regenerate.

The next time you're feeling stuck, remember the little toy novelty. Free your fingers by relaxing and giving in to your stuckness and they'll be turning out words for you in short order.

Post a reply: _____

_____

_____

_____

Post-Production

If you make a list of what happens during post-production, the process seems straightforward. The director and editor review the film shot during production and pull out the best takes and coverage. These are edited together according to the script and then the special effects, sound effects, and score are merged into the final film.

Peek behind the camera, though, and you'll discover that the watchwords in post-production are experimentation and flexibility. Directors and editors must remain open to new ways of working with the material they have. It might sound strange that at this point in the filmmaking process we're talking about changes and experiments. After all, everyone is working from the same script—the one that was approved months ago when the film went into pre-production.

Ah, yes; only that was before anyone took a good, hard look at those thousands of feet of film. As good as a script may be, it can only be a blueprint. What was written on the page may not work effectively on the screen. Post-production is the time when directors and editors discover the best way to tell the story.

The changes come about as 20 or 30 (or more) hours of film are whittled down into a 2-hour feature. It's a painstaking process, guided by experience and instinct. Whole sections of a film may have to be reconstructed to work with what's been shot. The order of scenes might change because what looked promising in the script is confusing, lackluster, or awkward on the screen. Perhaps the actors couldn't pull off a scene or the description on paper can't fully be realized on film.

Not until the structure of the film is established by the editor can the sound-effects specialists, the composer, the musicians, and the special-effects wizards fully utilize their talents and add the finishing touches audiences expect from a Hollywood movie. Even after their work's been completed, the movie is hardly complete. The film is screened repeatedly—for studio executives, marketing vice presidents, film bookers, and test audiences. Sequences that don't get the desired response, promote lapses in attention span, or create disconnects in story logic are rethought and, if necessary, reshot. Only then is the film ready to be evaluated by the real authorities, the audiences that vote with their dollar bills and credit cards.

Your path through post-production will mirror the one followed by the director and his team as they bring a film to life. Starting with your production draft you'll pull out the best takes and coverage, lay them out, get an idea of the flow of your essay, and see how what you envisioned as you shuffled your index cards looks as an essay. What you see may not look pretty. It's not supposed to. You'll have to maintain the same level of flexibility and experimentation as the director and editor. You'll move things around, reach back into your production draft for sentences and paragraphs you originally chose not to use, throw some words away, and write new ones to take their places. The only thing you can be sure of is that you will feel a bit unsure. That's natural. While the pre-production phase was full of order and logic and the production phase was full of free-flowing creativity, the post-production phase is a wild combination of the two.

While the posts in this chapter will help, there are no rules for moving merrily through the post-production transformation. Much of what happens in post-production happens through trial and error, and the results you get are a joint effort between your left and right brains. This time, your left brain takes the lead. During post-production you will need its critical thinking faculties. The left brain keeps the logic of the essay on track, asking questions such as "Does this make sense?" and "Does what I'm saying follow from what I just wrote?" The left brain will call upon your right brain to rewrite sentences and paragraphs to make the essay more visual and to add drama to your prose. On its own, your right brain will keep the left brain moving forward by asking the all-important question, "What happens next?"

Together, your left and right brains will get you through the post-production process—a process that is harrowing and frustrating, exhilarating and laugh-out-loud funny. At times post-production is plain hard work that separates people who think about writing from people like you: people who express their thoughts, ideas, and dreams in words.

Practice Nondestruction

Sometime in your life, perhaps even today, your mother told you to throw something away. Maybe something is an understatement. Maybe she's told you to throw everything away, under the guise of cleaning up your room. Think kindly of your mother. It's not her fault. The reason she thinks this way is that she's not a film editor and doesn't know one of the golden rules of editing: if you throw it away now, you will need it later.

Long before computers, film editors actually touched the film they edited. While frames of 35mm film are a whopping 1×1½ inches, editors in the 1930s and '40s worked with 16mm film in which each frame was about ¾ inch square. The good editors never tossed out a frame because they never knew when they were going to need it. It may be hard to believe that one frame carries so much weight, but editors will tell you that a single frame can make all the difference in the feel of a scene. So as editors snipped out and spliced together the pieces of film that made up the movie, they saved what they didn't use in metal bins—just in case.

While computers have saved editors from working with tiny bits of celluloid, film-editing software—from the programs used by the pros to the ones that come free on new laptops—never tosses unused frames away. These programs use a technique called non-destructive editing. Deleted frames hang around on the disk, they just don't show up in the film. If needed, they're only a few mouse clicks away.

When good writers hit post-production, they follow the same editing principle and never throw anything away. Once you irreversibly delete that sentence or paragraph, you might as well bet your college tuition that you'll want those words back. That's when you'll spend precious time reconstructing what you wrote and follow it with more precious time wondering whether you got the reconstruction right.

Put those creative thoughts to better use. Here are some tips for practicing nondestructive writing:

- Before you do anything else, make a backup copy of your production draft. To be on the safe side, set its properties to Read-Only so that you don't edit it by accident.

- Create a cuts file. Keep its window open on your desktop. Every time you cut something out of your essay, even if it's only a sentence, paste the cut into your cuts file. Separate each entry with a row of ==================.

- If you want to move an entry (or part of one) from your cuts file back to your essay, copy it rather than cut it. Your cuts file may wind up containing duplicate entries (if you later cut the entry again), but at least you know you'll always have your cuts if you need them.

- Create a notes file and keep its window open on your desktop, too. As you work on your essay, you'll think of things you want to do, add, or change. Write them in your notes file; anything from a few words to whole paragraphs. Review the contents of your notes file regularly for ideas you can use and improvements you can make.

While all this copying and pasting adds a little extra work to post-production, it's work you'll quickly forget about the first time you don't have to rewrite that deleted opening paragraph you want back. Be a good editor. Don't throw anything away.

But let's not mention it to your mother.

Post a reply: _____

_____

_____

_____

It's Your Choice

As you learn more about the steps involved in turning an idea into a feature film, you can begin to appreciate the number of decisions involved. From the choices made by the screenwriter to those made in the editing room, the cumulative number of decisions easily numbers in the thousands if not tens of thousands.

How can all those decisions get made?

Easy: one at a time. Often what's important is not the actual choice—the words used in a line of dialogue or the take selected for a particular scene—but making a choice in the first place. Once you make a choice, you can move forward, evaluate the results, and, if necessary, change your mind. While you are THINKING about what choice to make, your writing process is frozen in time—and frozen in time is just a polite name for feeling stuck, which is itself a polite way of describing writer's block.

"I don't have writer's block because I always go back to the idea that people have to make choices," says Steven Duncan. Now a professor of screenwriting at Loyola Marymount University in Los Angeles, Duncan co-created *Tour of Duty* for CBS. "Whenever I hit a block I ask myself what the options are—what's the best choice for a character or situation?" Duncan's method for avoiding stuckness is also one of the secrets for getting through post-production: keep on moving forward; keep on making choices.

"But wait," you say, "if I make the wrong choice, doesn't that mean I'm wasting my time? If I thought about what I was doing, I might make a better choice and not have to correct it later."

You're right. If you can avoid traveling down a road you will only have to retreat along later, by all means avoid it. This assumes, of course, that you know the road you want before you take it. When all roads look the same, what do you do?

Make a choice.

There's a story about a famous film director at the old MGM studios back in the days when MGM was known for its flashy, elaborate musicals. The director—often identified as Busby Berkeley, Vincente Minnelli, or Robert Z. Leonard (and, in truth, probably none of them)—came onto the set to watch the rehearsal of a big musical number. Instead, he found the dancers milling around talking, the pianist puffing on a cigarette, and the choreographer pacing the stage while holding his head in his hands.

"What's wrong?" the director asked.

"It's not working," said the choreographer.

"What's not working?"

"Everything," the choreographer said.

The director walked around the set and whispered instructions to each actor and dancer. He then nodded at the pianist, who proceeded to play the music for the number.

The director was no choreographer, and that was obvious as the dancers began to dance. Nobody did the same steps at the same time. Bodies bumped into each other on every beat. If the scene resembled anything, it was 3 gallons of fish trying to swim in a 1-gallon tank.

"Stop, stop," said the choreographer.

"Why?" said the director.

"It's awful." Whereupon the choreographer listed what each dancer was doing wrong.

"Excellent," said the director. "Now that you know what's wrong, you can fix it."

That's the way it is in post-production. As long as the dancers aren't moving, you have nothing to fix. Once you get them moving, you can see what needs to be done.

Making choices is how you get the dancers moving.

Post a reply: _____

_____

_____

_____

The Accidental Filmmaker

Nothing in a film happens by accident.

By the time a film opens in your neighborhood theater, every frame has been seen and scrutinized by producers, associate producers, assistant producers, assistants to the producers, editors, negative cutters, preview audiences, interns, audio engineers, Foley artists, wives, husbands, mistresses, limo drivers, and the star's mother. Every detail in every frame is there because someone, or groups of someones, decided it belonged. Even mistakes, or what appear to be mistakes, are there because somebody decided, for whatever reason, it was better to leave the mistakes in than to fix them.

When people read essays, they make the same assumption. Everything in your essay is there because you wanted it to be. Naturally, poor grammar and punctuation fall into this category. Beyond the mechanics of English, your reader assumes that the words, sentences, and ideas are there for a reason. So should you. When you describe the Constitution as "unique" rather than "revolutionary," your reader assumes you thought about the difference and approved the distinction.

This is why submitting your first draft—your production draft—as a finished product or assignment is a foolish action. During production, your right brain is in charge. Making sure you have the best words, sentences, and ideas is a left-brain function. Your left brain takes the place of all those people whispering advice and warnings into the director's ear. Post-production is the time to turn your left brain loose. You'll get valuable advice, but only if you take the time to hear it.

Post-production gives you the opportunity to parade your essay in front of the dozens of eyes that are your left brain and to make sure that all your essay's words, sentences, thoughts, and ideas are no accident.

Post a reply: _____

_____

_____

_____

Tick, Tick, Tick

Is there a time bomb in your DVD collection?

The chances are good you've got one in there, especially if your taste in movies includes any of the big action films. In all or in part, many of these films include what's known as the ticking time bomb. The hero has a finite amount of time to save the world, or a big part thereof, from destruction. Sometimes the plot involves a real ticking bomb, such as a rogue nuclear device. Other times, the ticking bomb is a metaphor. The aliens will attack in two hours. The meteor will collide with Earth in three days. The kidnappers will kill the hostage if the ransom isn't paid in 30 minutes.

Film audiences know the hero will prevail because that's part of the Hollywood formula. Audiences come to see how the hero will beat the odds, so that journey must be as exciting as possible. In a heart-stopping thriller, nothing comes easy. Every time the hero has the upper hand, somebody switches hands. Every time the hero sees a clear path to victory, someone parks an 18-wheeler in the way. Tick, tick, tick.

As the deadline for your essay looms, you will find your writing process has to zig and zag to get you where you want to be. Rarely will you sit down and rewrite or polish your essay in order, start to finish. More than likely, you'll work on a support point and then the opening won't work. You'll fix the opening and the ending will fall flat. You'll rewrite the ending and now the support point leading into it will seem off. One student described the process as akin to nailing Jell-O to a tree.

What do you do?

You do what any hero does. You solve the problem in front of you, then tick it off your list. One problem after another—tick, tick, tick.

Post a reply: _____

_____

_____

_____

If at First You Don't Succeed, Make Another Mistake

When Tom was a film student at Loyola Marymount University, he took a class in film editing. For his final project, he had to edit a fight scene from *Gunsmoke*, the iconic television western from the 1950s. Part of the scene included a shot of townspeople watching the fight. Tom included a few seconds of that shot because it felt right to him. What he learned about those few seconds will help you with your writing.

When he showed the final edit to his professor, the prof watched it carefully, stroked his chin, and said, "Fix the shot of the spectators."

"How?" Tom said. The shot seemed fine to him.

"Take out some frames at the end. It's too much looking."

Dutifully, Tom removed a few frames, each a piece of film about ¾ inch square and each representing only ¹⁄₂₄ of a second of screen time.

"Too short on the spectators," Tom's professor said when Tom showed him the re-edit. Tom returned to the editing room and added back a few of the frames he'd cut out. When the professor looked at this next version, he didn't even have to speak. Tom could see it in his eyes. "Too much?" Tom asked. His professor nodded.

Back Tom slinked to the editing room, where he chased film frames around a table, ¾-inch squares that would fly away if you looked at them incorrectly, each one bound in place by increasing layers of sticky, transparent tape. Through the sheer process of elimination—Tom had never edited a piece of film in his life—he struck the right length for the spectator shot, a fact his professor acknowledged with a grudging grunt.

"Hold on," Tom said, "all that work hardly seems worth it. In fact, it seems kind of arbitrary."

"Go back and shorten the spectator shot by one frame," the professor said.

Tom did, cursing as he peeled sticky tape off the film and angry at himself for not keeping his mouth shut. Tom made the edit and was hardly prepared for what he saw.

There was something wrong with the spectator shot.

Tom couldn't describe it. All he knew was that the moment didn't feel right. It's that same feeling you have when you're coming down with a cold but you don't know it. You feel off center, but there's nothing specific to put your finger on. That's how the spectator shot felt.

On a whim, Tom lengthened the original shot by a frame. The feeling was slightly different, but the result was the same. There was something wrong.

"It comes with experience," was all his professor offered by way of explanation as to how he knew the optimal length for the shot. The lesson Tom learned was that sometimes the only way to find what works is to eliminate what doesn't.

Jeffrey Davis, playwright, former sitcom writer, and now the chair of the screenwriting program at Loyola Marymount University in Los Angeles, can relate to the process. "I've probably written more things wrong than anybody you'll ever meet."

Not exactly the kind of admission you'd expect from a writer accustomed to seeing his work on television and on stage.

"Everybody, including me, is going to write badly the first time out. I don't mean when you're a kid. I mean your first draft of anything is going to be bad. And you should embrace that," Davis says.

Post-production is the time to embrace your mistakes. As you edit your essay, move words, sentences, and paragraphs around; play with support points; try various introductions and conclusions; and make as many mistakes as you can. Not mistakes in usage or spelling, but mistakes that make you think, "Oh, that doesn't work." Then ask yourself why it doesn't work. Does the essay seem choppy? Does it wander around the point? Does your latest support point seem unconvincing? Perhaps you've already made your point and your additions seem anticlimactic. Juggle your essay around, a frame at a time, until it just feels right.

Consider this post a free pass. It's your permission to screw up during post-production.

Post a reply: _____

_____

_____

_____

Rough Cut

As the first step in post-production, a film's editor usually creates what's called a rough cut.

To construct a rough cut, the editor grabs a copy of the script and works through all the takes, making educated guesses about which ones to include. What comes out of the editing suite is choppy and awkwardly un-film-like. There are no fades, dissolves, music, sound effects, or fancy graphics. But a rough cut is enough to give the director and producers a feel for how the story will look as a movie before anybody invests time and energy in precision editing, fades, dissolves, music, sound effects, and fancy graphics. Creating a rough cut of your essay might conserve your time and energy, too.

A word of caution: the writing rough cut isn't for everyone. You may find that the smoothness and flow of more polished writing helps you sort out the good and the bad in your work. "I usually polish the first 30 pages of my screenplay until I'm happy with it. Until I do that, I can't move on," says Jeff Wynne, a feature film and animation screenwriter. If that's the way you write, excellent. Use that method because it works for you.

But if you find yourself frustrated because you keep losing your place in your writing, or you don't see the big picture because you're always bogged down in details, or you find that the pieces of your essay never seem to fit together no matter how well writ-ten they are, a rough cut might be your best solution. A rough cut is your first chance to see your argument laid out in front of you since pre-production, when you were working with your index cards. The card view was for you. Now you'll look at your essay through your reader's eyes.

Assemble your rough cut the way film editors assemble theirs. Scan your production draft and select what you feel are your best takes and coverage. Cut and paste everything else to your cuts file (see "Practice Nondestruction," page 116). Read your production draft from the beginning until you discover where your essay starts (see "Finding the Slap," page 144). Move everything before the start to your cuts file, too. Remember, this is only an educated guess about what belongs in your essay. It's all right if you're not sure whether this material should be part of the final version.

Once you have your rough cut assembled, here are some questions to ask yourself:

- Does your essay build? Does it start small and grow increasingly more convincing?

- Do you contradict yourself? Are support points making competing claims? Does one point weaken any of the others?

- Is your thesis clearly stated early in your essay (certainly on the first page and preferably by the end of your second paragraph)?

- Do your support points relate back to your thesis, or do some introduce ideas that support a different argument?

- Do your support points argue both sides of your thesis instead of just the one you are trying to prove?

- Have you included only one take for each support point? Multiple takes are not multiple support points, they're the same support point written multiple ways.

- Does your conclusion show how the body of your essay proves your thesis?

- Does your conclusion tie up any loose ends?

Accept that your first efforts will be ugly. Thoughts may not flow smoothly from one to another. Ideas may repeat themselves. Sentences may ramble on or sound stilted and artificial. Your argument may seem full of holes. This is exactly why a rough cut is worth the extra time and energy.

It's disappointing and frustrating to polish your way through the first half of your essay only to run into a snag in the middle. Suddenly, you realize you have to tear apart all that carefully polished prose. A rough cut reduces the chances of getting caught in that situation because you're not rewriting, you're cutting and pasting your way to a quick overview of your literary landscape. Once you feel comfortable with the overall flow, you're ready to tackle a more crafted version.

Making a rough cut can't guarantee you won't encounter problems later on. Discovering and fixing problems is part of the process in both filmmaking and writing. However, as film editors and many writers will tell you, starting with a rough cut can lead to a smooth finish.

Post a reply: _____

_____

_____

_____

Choosing Takes and Coverage

"I look for the best performances, the ones that seem to belong in the film at that moment. I start there, even though I know what I select may not make the final cut." That's the way film editor J. D. Ryan describes his process for whittling down the thousands of feet of film shot by his director into a full-length movie.

Ryan's words echo the advice from other editors and directors who also begin by looking for the best takes and coverage, fully aware that the best shots are not the best by themselves but are the best when combined with all the other best shots. Every moment in a movie works because it works with every other moment.

In post-production, you'll discover the same holds true for your essay. As you whittle down your production draft into a finished piece of writing, every sentence in your essay will work because it works with every other sentence.

"But wait," you say, "if everything depends on everything else, where do I start? How do I know what to choose?"

Congratulations for asking, because you have identified another of the great secrets of writing. Writing, like filmmaking, is made up of hundreds of tiny steps of trial and error. There is no mystical rule for finding where to begin, no magic formula for finding the best take. It's just as well. Rules and formulas do only one thing: they help you write like the person who wrote the rules and formulas rather than the person who writes like you. Part of finding your writing process is creating those rules and formulas on your own.

Since there's no method for finding the right take, the best
this post can do is give you a sense of what you're looking for.
Remember: the guidelines that follow are only guidelines. With
experience you'll become better at spotting takes that work, and
don't work, in your writing. The only way to get that experience is
by experimenting with different takes in your essays.

- If all else is equal, pick a take that expresses your thought or
  makes your point in the fewest words. Sometimes you need
  some extra words to provide the proper rhythm to your writing, but in general, early drafts almost always contain more
  words than necessary.

- Pick a take whose pacing complements the point you are
  making (see "How to Score," page 186). Short, sharp sentences typically emphasize the importance or drama of
  what you are writing. Longer sentences typically emphasize the descriptive qualities, including facts and details.
  Here's an example. Compare "The general erred. His men
  were well armed but completely exposed. The mistake cost
  him his command. It nearly cost us the war," to "The general
  erred by ordering his men into the open plain. Though they
  were armed with rifles, handguns, and several horse-drawn
  cannons, their surroundings offered no cover. Completely
  exposed, the soldiers were no match for the well-hidden
  enemy, and the slaughter that ensued cost the general his
  command and nearly cost us the war." Both passages make
  the same points, but with different pacing and emphasis.

- If all else is equal, pick the take or coverage that creates the best visual image (see "Picture This," page 53; "On Location in Mary Land," page 165; and "I've Got a Question," page 46). Sometimes this guideline seems to conflict with the one about picking the shortest take. The key words here are "if all else is equal." Search for the take that creates the best visual image with the fewest words. For example, "I hate my new cell phone. It's an ugly, battery-sucking brick," instead of "I hate my new cell phone. It needs to be charged every couple hours. It's heavy. It doesn't even look cool."

Whether you find your best takes or best coverage waiting for you as you read your production draft or whether you create them by combining parts from different takes (see "Make a Scene," page 139), remember that any choice you make is your best guess at what works at the moment you make it. Be prepared to change your mind as you work through post-production, no matter how much teeth-gnashing, knuckle-cracking, or creative cursing went into a support point, paragraph, or sentence. For the good of your essay (not to mention your teeth, knuckles, and your relationship with your parents) if what you have doesn't work, rewrite or replace it.

Whether a take is good, bad, right, wrong, in, or out is a choice you have to make. And, if at first you don't succeed, join the club.

Post a reply: _____

_____

_____

_____

Why Leonardo DiCaprio Doesn't Go to the Bathroom

Inception, starring Leonardo DiCaprio, is another film by Christopher Nolan in which he creates believable worlds out of dreams and memories. The film's story spans months—if not years—and during that time, Cobb, DiCaprio's character, never goes to the bathroom.

Come to think of it, Jack Bauer, Kiefer Sutherland's character in the television show *24,* went for an entire day every season without a potty break. (He also never needed to charge his cell phone.)

What's the story?

Is superhuman bladder control a prerequisite for becoming an action hero? (And do you have to buy your cell phone batteries from a secret CIA lab hidden in a cornfield outside of Norman, Oklahoma?)

If you answered, "Who cares?" to all this dribble, you are 100 percent correct. Who cares, indeed? Leonardo DiCaprio, Kiefer Sutherland, Bruce Lee, and even John Wayne don't go to the bathroom in their films because bathroom breaks aren't relevant to their stories. Unless a character's presence in a bathroom has something to do with moving the story forward, watching that character hit the head, visit the loo, tap a kidney, or make a pit stop won't show up on any director's shot list.

Nor will any other scenes that aren't part of what filmmakers recognize as cause and effect.

Let's cut to a scene in a bar. The joint is crowded with hardly a place to stand, let alone sit. At one end of the bar, a suave young man—clearly a legend in his own mind—is elbowing his way in between an attractive, unaccompanied woman and a serious-looking bear of a man who's on his third mug of beer.

Mr. Suave hits on Ms. Unaccompanied and she shoots him down. He tries again; she turns her back. This time, he rolls out his best pick-up line, and she walks away. Angry and disgusted, Mr. Suave pounds his fist on the bar. Mr. Bear of a Man is so startled he knocks his beer into his lap. After looking at his damp pants, Mr. Bear looks for the person responsible and, spotting Mr. Suave, Mr. Bear lifts all of his 6-foot, 10-inch frame off his bar stool and doubles his fists. In the interest of family entertainment, we'll cut away right here—but suffice it to say that when he arrives home, Mr. Suave hardly looks that way.

What happened in this scene is an example of cause and effect.

Mr. Suave hit on Ms. Unaccompanied (cause). She shot him down (effect). This only made him try again (cause) and get shot down again (effect). He tried a third time (cause) and she left (effect), which made him angry (cause); he pounded the bar (effect), which startled Mr. Bear (cause) and resulted in his spilling his beer (effect), and so on.

Each event had an effect that also was a cause leading to another event. What sets a story apart from merely a list of events that happened to a character on a given day is this: the events in a story are linked together by a chain of cause and effect.

Change "event" to "scene" and you can see that the process of choosing scenes to include in a movie is dominated by cause and effect. No matter how brilliant the performances, how clever the dialogue, or how sparkling the cinematography, if a scene doesn't contribute to the film's chain of cause and effect, it never leaves the editing room.

(If you'd like to see what happens when you tamper with cause and effect, watch *Run Lola Run,* the 1998 film by German writer-director Tom Tykwer.)

Change "scene" to "paragraph" and you have yet another way of deciding which of your takes to keep in your essay and which to send to your cut file (see "Choosing Takes and Coverage," page 132; and "Practice Nondestruction," page 116). If a paragraph isn't part of your essay's cause-and-effect chain, out it goes—even if it's the best piece of writing you've ever done in your life. (Don't worry; it's not. Life is a long, long time.)

What's an essay's chain of cause and effect? It's the logical steps between thesis and proof. If a paragraph in your essay doesn't move your reader one step closer to understanding why your thesis is true, that sentence is wasting your reader's time.

Making these cuts during post-production can be a gut-wrenching task. Tom McLoughlin knows that firsthand. In his early days, McLoughlin directed *Jason Lives: Friday the 13th Part VI.* Today, his writing and directing credits include scores of television movies and feature films. Even a pro like McLoughlin occasionally comes face to face with a brilliant scene that just doesn't belong.

"Sometimes there's a scene you feel is absolutely crucial so you stick it into the movie. Then you watch the movie back, and you come to that scene, and it's like, 'What happened to the story?' or 'Who put the brakes on?'" says McLoughlin.

That's when a good director knows it's time for the hard decision.

"There are times you have to say, 'I know how much the scene cost to shoot. I know the producer is going to kill me …' Nevertheless, out it goes."

What can you do during production to avoid having to make these cuts in post-production? Not much.

"You can't predict it," says McLoughlin. "I wish I could. Crying 'uncle' is always horribly difficult."

Since you can't avoid it, you have to learn to deal with it. Ask yourself whether a paragraph, a sentence, or even a word moves your essay one link further along the chain from thesis to proof. If it does, keep it.

If not, give what you wrote its own bathroom break and flush it.

Post a reply: _____

_____

_____

_____

Make a Scene

Even if you've never been on a film set, you probably know what sticks are. Perhaps you don't know the name, but you've seen sticks in films, television shows, and commercials that show glimpses of behind-the-scenes Hollywood production. Remember that little chalkboard with the moveable arm on top? Someone yells, "Scene one, take three," a hand snaps the arm down with a CLACK and pulls the contraption out of the frame.

That contraption? Sticks.

Sticks serve several purposes, one of which is identifying each take so the editor can tell one from the other. Of course, the sticks are edited out of a film, but if they weren't, you'd see that most scenes were constructed from little parts of many takes. Filmmaking folklore would like you to believe that actors deliver their lines perfectly as a magic camera dances around them, always capturing the actors' best sides on film. In reality, what appears to be a single sentence spoken by a single actor may actually be made up of two sentences from different takes cobbled together in post-production to achieve the best results.

Editors talk all the time about making performances, which is their way of saying they assemble the best parts of different takes into a scene that appears to be a single, flawless one. You can do that, too. Where editors combine frames from different takes, you combine words. Remember the objective here is to get something that works in your essay—the best performance, as it were. You should feel free to assemble the best parts of your takes into a single paragraph, sentence, or even a phrase that appears to have flowed, flawlessly, from your fingers.

This illusion of flawless performance doesn't belong only to Hollywood. It's completely appropriate for your writing as well.

Post a reply: _____

_____

_____

_____

Start at the Slap

Once again it's time for you to step into the role of a Hollywood director. You're in post-production for your major motion picture, *Hate—A Love Story,* and your editor has spliced together a sequence for your review. Here's what we see as the editor plays the sequence on his computer.

A man in a small, sparsely decorated apartment dials his cell phone.

Cut to a larger apartment that is decorated with stylistic flair on a budget. A woman, a little younger than the man and smartly dressed, answers her cell phone. Cut back to the man. He says something into the phone.

Cut to the woman. She responds with a scowl.

Cut to the man. He responds in kind before saying something else.

Cut to the woman. She's scowling more and shaking her fist at her phone as well.

Cut to the man. He's pacing, yelling into his phone, waving his free arm about the apartment.

Cut to the woman as she says something into her phone before flinging it onto the sofa.

Cut to the man as he stuffs the phone in his pocket, throws a jacket around his shoulders, and bolts through the front door, slamming it behind him.

Cut to the hallway outside the woman's apartment as the man rings the doorbell with fervor. The woman opens the door and the man storms in.

Cut to inside the woman's apartment. The man closes the door behind him and stands in front of it. The woman is on the other side of the room. She wags her finger at him while saying some unkind words.

The man's eyes grow wide. He marches toward her, matching her words in kind until they are nose to nose.

He utters the magic words, whatever they are, and she slaps him.

Somewhat reflexively, he slaps her back.

She retreats to a corner of the room where she picks up a vase and throws it at him.

He ducks. The vase shatters against the wall.

She picks up a framed picture from an end table and fires another strike. He ducks again as the frame hits the wall—one fewer framed picture in the world. But he has to act quickly because she lets fly a decorative plate in his direction.

He's not waiting around. He ducks low, opens the door, and beats a hasty retreat.

Whew.

The editor's thoughts, exactly. "It's too long, isn't it?" he says. You nod in agreement. "Okay, then, where would you like this to start?"

That's your challenge. There's a starting point in there some-place. You knew it when you saw the script. You knew it when you shot the sequence. But now in post-production you have to find it. What's your call? At what specific moment do you want this sequence to begin, and why? Take a few minutes to think what you would tell your editor.

In my workshops, responses stretch all the way from starting at the slap to starting where the sequence begins now. While students may not agree on where to begin, they almost always agree where not to begin. Rarely does anyone suggest starting after the slap.

Why?

The slap is the first moment in the sequence that conveys all the emotion and conflict that precedes it. Not only that, the description of the slap frequently elicits gasps from the students. The slap not only summarizes everything we need to know about these people and their relationship, it evokes an emotional response— in this case, surprise, shock, or disgust—as well. In one instant, the slap gets everybody's attention and provides enough information so everyone can make sense out of what happens next.

For this reason, start this sequence at the slap.

In the film business, writers want to begin their scenes when the action is underway—when audiences can get a picture of what's happened before by watching what's happening now. Writers call this starting *en media res,* a Latin phrase meaning "in the middle of things." You can call it starting at the slap.

Where's the slap in your essay?

Post a reply: _____

_____

_____

_____

Finding the Slap

A movie's first few moments better make you curious or you'll know buying a ticket was a mistake before the opening music fades away. Similarly, an essay that fails to make your reader curious probably won't get read. If your reader HAS to read your essay—because she's your teacher, counselor, or college application evaluator—chances are she's already lowered her expectation of being interested in what you have to say. That's why in an earlier post (see "Start at the Slap," page 141) I wrote about the importance of starting your essay at the slap.

"But wait," you say, "I read that post, and I still wouldn't recognize a slap if it walked up and hit me in the face." Well, before you turn the other cheek and walk away, do what editors do in post-production. Run a scene forward from the beginning and stop at the slap. For you, that means picking up your production draft and reading it from the beginning. Stop at the moment you first become interested in what you wrote.

Chances are, you stopped at a place that raised a mystery, set forth a problem or warning, or created an incongruity but most of all left you curious and asking yourself, "What happened and what happens next?"

Congratulations. You've found your slap.

Still not sure you found what you're looking for? Let's see how to recognize a good slap by looking at the slaps directors and editors pull out in post-production to grab your attention from the first frame:

- Incongruity—Something happens that goes against what we know, expect, or believe to be normal. For example, in *Goldfinger*, James Bond emerges from the ocean in full Scuba gear. He peels off his wet suit to reveal he's wearing a (totally dry) tuxedo.

- Mystery—In *Field of Dreams*, a disembodied voice (in the middle of a cornfield, no less) advises Iowa farmer Ray Kinsella, "If you build it, he will come."

- Action—A dramatic recreation of D-Day assaults the senses the way the Allies assault Omaha Beach at the opening of *Saving Private Ryan*.

- Danger or warning—In *Invictus*, as he watches the presidential motorcade go by, a high-school soccer coach turns to one of his students and says that he should remember today as the day the country (South Africa) went to the dogs.

- Problem—Edward Lewis, the rich, ruthless businessman in *Pretty Woman*, needs driving directions to Beverly Hills. Vivian Ward, a Hollywood prostitute, needs rent money. Maybe Edward and Vivian can help each other out.

This is not an exhaustive list, and the categories overlap, but the techniques are some of the most popular in Hollywood's repertoire. All these slaps have something in common. They start in the middle of the action and, by doing so, leave you pondering two questions: what happened and what happens next? When you open your essay, a good slap leaves your reader with the same thoughts.

Just to make sure you'll know a slap when you come face to face with it, let's practice writing an opening slap for an essay topic that makes the rounds in schools every few years: the question of whether Shakespeare actually wrote all the plays attributed to him. Some scholars claim they have found proof, by analyzing Shakespeare's works and the writings of his contemporaries, that Francis Bacon wrote some of the plays that bear Shakespeare's name. Write a slap for an essay that argues just that. In fact, write several opening slaps, one for each of the categories (incongruity, mystery, action, problem, danger or warning). Only then take a look at the following student examples:

- Incongruity: The sixteenth-century author, scribbling Hamlet's next line with a quill pen, hardly looked like William Shakespeare.

- Mystery: As the curtain fell on the first-ever performance of *Hamlet,* only one man in the theater knew who rightly deserved the applause of the crowd.

- Action: "It's mine," said the famous author.

  "No, it's not," said the famous poet.

- Problem: Shakespeare has made heroes out of some scholars and fools out of others.

- Danger: Be careful about what you think you know about literary history.

- Danger: Signing my name to this paper took courage.

- Problem: I spent hours wondering whether to sign my name to this paper.

How did you do? Do your slaps start your reader wondering what happened and what happens next? If not, try writing some new ones. Now that you know what a slap looks and feels like, return to the top of your production draft, start reading, and stop at the slap.

Move it to the start of your essay where it belongs. You don't have to be curious about your slap any longer.

Now it's your reader's turn.

Post a reply: _____

_____

_____

_____

Hammocking

Most movies open big. Action/adventure films almost always begin big. Even films that seem to open small open big. Orson Welles's *Touch of Evil* begins with a single, continuous shot (no cuts or edits) that rapidly becomes a visual ballet, dwarfing the action and dialogue. Similarly, most films end big. Ending big doesn't mean fading out on an exploding supernova, it means ending with a memorable or emotional moment.

We tend to remember film beginnings and endings even while their middles fade. Scholars who study stories and storytelling will tell you this effect is a result of the way beginnings and endings are inextricably linked. We need the ending to make sense of the beginning, which, when we first encounter it, seems to come out of nowhere. Only after we reach the end of the story do we think back to its beginning and realize what was going on. Somewhere in that process the poor middle gets overlooked.

Filmmakers use this selective amnesia to their advantage. In post-production, they'll put a slower, less-memorable scene between two knock-your-socks-off sequences. Even within a scene, editors have a sixth sense about arranging moments with much talk and little action in between big, emotional moments that blot the weak middle out of your mind.

The neglected middle works to your advantage, too, as you order your support points during post-production.

Most of the time, your reader will remember your first and last support points with the greatest clarity. When you order your support points in your essay, hang your weaker ones between the strongest two. This doesn't mean you can get away with a handful of lame support points because you found a couple of zingers. All your support points should be strong. Some, however, will be stronger than others. You might want to think of the first and last support points as posts (as in fence posts, not blog posts) with the remaining, middle support points hanging between them, much the way one puts up a hammock.

Hence the term hammocking.

As you'll see, there's a trick to placing those posts in your essay. First, though, you need to rank your support points from strongest to weakest. Make a list on paper, index cards, or your computer, using short phrases to summarize the key idea in each point. What you're looking for is how powerful and convincing you believe each point to be. (For some suggestions, see "Elevator Pitch," page 151.)

Now for that trick. Once you have your list of support points ranked from strongest to weakest, lead with the support point that's SECOND on your list. Finish with your strongest one. Keep your weakest support point in the middle. If you have more than 3 support points—let's say you have 5—where 5 is the strongest and 1 the weakest, use the same strategy. Try an arrangement such as 4, 2, 1, 3, 5, which takes your weakest point and flanks it with stronger ones.

Your two strongest points support most of the weight while the others rest between them.

All that's missing in this hammock is some sunshine and lemonade.

Post a reply: _____

_____

_____

_____

Elevator Pitch

As you work through post-production, you're going to want to assemble your support points in an order that leaves little doubt that your argument is 100 percent solid (see "Hammocking," page 148). Your first step is identifying your strongest and weakest points. Here's a technique for ranking your support points. It comes from a mind game played by screenwriters and producers who are pitching films to studio executives.

The game is called the elevator pitch.

The idea is to come up with a description of your project you can pitch to a studio head while riding in an elevator. Since all you know about the elevator ride is that it will be brief (perhaps only 30 seconds), your pitch has to be short and persuasive.

We're going to use the concept of an elevator pitch to sort through your support points and put them in order of persuasiveness. Your first step is to write a one- or two-sentence summary of each support point. You can do this on index cards, a sheet of paper, or a file on your computer. You don't have to be fancy here; this isn't a creative writing contest or an English quiz. Just capture the essence of the support point—what you might say to someone who is in a hurry (or in an elevator) and only wants to hear the bottom line.

Now it's time for some acting. Imagine you are that stern, skeptical teacher, the one who questions everything. You know who I'm talking about—the one you'd have a hard time convincing about the existence of gravity. There you are, you as you, in an elevator. It stops on the second floor, and in walks you as the teacher. The doors close behind you.

YOU AS TEACHER: Well, what have you got to say for yourself?

YOU AS YOU: (Here's where you fire off your first support point.)

Are you as teacher convinced? Extremely convinced? Somewhat convinced? So skeptical your eyebrows arch and hit the mirrored ceiling of the elevator car?

Quickly score that support point from 1 (a dud) to 10 (a miracle). Continue through your support point list until you've scored them all. Now rank them from strongest to weakest as you prepare to choose the ones that will grace your essay. If two points have the same score, flip a coin to break the tie. In the event of a multiple-way tie, go back to the elevator. You're just not being skeptical enough.

Once you have your support points ordered, you can step out of the elevator and back into the real world. And don't push all the floor buttons on the way out.

Post a reply: _____

_____

_____

_____

Getting from Point A to Point B

Here's the beginning of an experimental movie. See what you think.

The sun rises over a volcano. A small airplane circles the volcano, barely skipping above the top.

Cut to inside the airplane. A man and woman, both dressed in khaki shirts, sit next to each other. He's at the controls. She's taking pictures out the side window, carefully balancing her camera, with its long telephoto lens, as the plane is buffeted by the updrafts around the volcano.

"Hold this thing still, will you?" she says.

"Anytime you think you can do a better job, you're welcome to try," he says.

Cut to the inside of a modern office. Lots of glass windows set off a sleek chrome desk. A woman sits behind the desk. She wears a navy blue suit, white blouse, red shoes, and a red scarf. She swivels her chair to look at the windows behind her, which are covered with 8 by 10 photographs of the volcano. A man stands in front of the desk.

An off-screen voice says, "Meanwhile, in a modern downtown office building, Janice and Dave are having a conversation about the volcano."

"They don't know they're doomed, do they?" the man says.

She turns slowly back to face him. "They will never get in the way of my plans again," she says. The man nods.

Cut to the inside of the small plane. The bouncing and shaking are worse than before.

The same off-screen voice says, "More importantly, Sarah and Harry are unaware of the danger they're in."

"We should get paid double for this assignment," the woman says.

"We will," says the man. "I've got that dame wrapped around my little finger."

How do you like the experiment, the off-screen voice telling you where you are and what's going on? Isn't it … what's the word …?

Weird?

What possible need could there be for a mysterious voice telling us we've moved from one scene to another? Meanwhile, the same kind of help we don't need in movies crops up repeatedly in essays. Most importantly, we see it in paragraphs that begin with transitional words and phrases such as *meanwhile* and *most importantly,* along with *similarly, for the most part, furthermore, moreover,* and *in the meantime.*

Why are these transitions so popular in writing, but we make fun of similar transitions in movies? The answer lies in the way movies are constructed.

If you study a film scene you'll discover it's put together like a miniature movie. A movie has a beginning, middle, and end. So does a scene. A movie begins with a slap (see "Start at the Slap," page 141). So does a scene. A movie identifies its characters, what they want, and what the story is about in the first few moments.

So does a scene. Because scenes are designed to orient us in the story, most movies can make transitions from one scene to the next with simple cuts.

That's what makes the off-screen voice superfluous, if not ridiculous.

You'll find that if you start your support points at their slaps and orient your reader at the start of each point, the way a movie does, then a simple cut with no transition will carry you from one support point to another most of the time.

What about the other times?

Watch movies closely and you'll also notice that, in addition to cuts, there are two other transitions filmmakers use. One is a dissolve. The current scene fades out as the next scene fades in. You probably know what that means: some length of time has passed between the two scenes. When a longer period of time has passed, a filmmaker will use a fade out followed by a fade in. Fades are similar to dissolves, except fades leave a period of black between the two scenes. The more black, the longer the leap in time.

Use a transition in your essay to warn your reader of a gap—not in time but in logic. For example, you might want to switch from a point that supports your thesis to one that doesn't, so you can expose the flaws in a counterargument. You can preface the second support point with a short transition. "Unfortunately, not everyone believes …," or "On the other hand …," will help your reader follow what might otherwise be mistaken for a reversal in your thinking.

Your production draft is probably full of transitions. That's fine. One of the benefits of transitions is that they allow you to keep the words flowing instead of worrying whether one paragraph (or sentence) leads into the next. In post-production, it's time to see just how many of those transitions you need.

Furthermore, the post "Making the Cut" (page 157) will help you do just that. For the most part.

Post a reply: _____

_____

_____

_____

Making the Cut

Most of the posts in this book stand on their own. This isn't one of them. Before you read this post, be sure you read "Getting from Point A to Point B" on page 153.

Transitions seem to make your writing flow smoothly, but most of the time they are a warning that an important part of your story didn't make it onto the page. Here's an example. Imagine you're writing a personal essay, one you might include as part of a college application. You're answering a question about an important lesson you learned, and your story involves a major disagreement with your parents. You've written:

> I had a fight with my parents, got up from the table, and went to my room. At the same time, my parents finished dinner. They never apologized.

The transition, "At the same time" isn't necessary. You can see this for yourself by rewriting the passage without it.

> I went to my room. My parents finished dinner. They never apologized.

There's no confusion about when your parents finished eating. They finished after you went to your room. Absent any information to the contrary, readers assume that the two events follow each other in time. Nevertheless, "At the same time ..." seems to add something. Without it, the story seems too abrupt, too matter-of-fact. If the phrase doesn't clarify the time relationship, what does it do?

While in movies transitions cover up gaps in time, transitions in essays typically cover up missing details. What is "At the same time ..." hiding? Let's find out by expanding the story.

You went to your room. You were angry. Your parents didn't care. You waited for an apology. Your parents finished eating. You grew angrier, they grew fuller. That's what you're writing about.

"At the same time ..." substitutes for, "And while I was in my room getting angry, my parents were stuffing their faces at dinner and not caring enough about me to apologize." Only "At the same time ..." doesn't say any of that. It weakly implies that something was happening while you're in your room, a something more effectively described by:

> I had a fight with my parents, got up from the table, and locked myself in my room for hours. My parents calmly finished dinner, laughing and talking, and the apology I deserved never came.

"But wait," you say, "doesn't 'At the same time ...' add emphasis to my parents eating dinner, making it more important?"

Fair enough. Your parents' behavior is important to your story. The behavior is so important it shouldn't be trusted to a transition, which rarely paints a visual image (see "Picture This," page 53; "On Location in Mary Land," page 165; and "I've Got a Question," page 46). To make your parents' behavior stand out on the page, we can use the same trick Hollywood filmmakers rely on to make something stand out on the screen.

Shine light on it.

We can shine light on something in our writing by providing more details about it. Let's bathe your parents' insensitive behavior in enough illumination to make it, as they say in Hollywood, pop.

> I had a fight with my parents, got up from the table, and locked myself in my room for hours. My parents calmly finished dinner. They laughed and talked. They chewed and swallowed. They had second helpings and thirds. They did everything but give me the apology I deserved.

See how your parents' actions become the focus of the tension between your sulking in your room and their enjoying themselves at the table? Their actions are illuminated in a way "At the same time ..." can never achieve.

As you work through your production draft, here are some tips for deciding whether a transition helps or hurts your essay:

- Assemble your essay, leaving in any transitions you feel are necessary.

- Remove the transition and see if the writing still works. If so, move on. If not, ask yourself what gap the transition is covering up. If it's a jump in logic or time, the transition should probably remain. If it's covering up a missing part of your story, write the missing part.

- Sometimes, the missing part of your story comes BEFORE the transition. Check to see that the end of the previous support point truly ends that point by tying it back to your thesis. If it doesn't, you may be depending on the transition to do that for you. In this case, the missing part of your story is the ending of the previous support point.

During production, transitions help you quickly slide from one thought to another so you keep moving forward. In post-production, transitions warn you that you may have skipped over or abbreviated parts of your story. Once you've added the missing pieces, the transition has done its job. Thank it, remove it, and proceed to the next one.

Post a reply: _____

_____

_____

_____

Reaching the Right Conclusion

By the time the final moments of *Avatar* unwind on the screen, the film has already settled the question of who lives, who dies, and who wins the battle for the planet. So what is there left to tell us? Despite the commercialism involved (the last scene of *Avatar* sets us up for the sequel), the final moment of the film makes a statement about the future of the two lead characters. Director James Cameron is capitalizing on another secret that screenwriters and filmmakers know: that we believe characters have adventures and experiences after the closing credits. We want to know what happens to them now that we have invested two hours living their lives. We don't want their stories to end. This is why the most memorable film endings tend to be ones that both sum up the story and offer a glimpse—usually a hopeful glimpse—into the future, assuring us there is more to come.

Endings like these don't just happen. Often they are crafted during post-production to make sure that the look and feel of the ending—its pacing, timing, lighting, and emotional energy—convey that magical sense of finality and future.

You can make your conclusions more memorable by following Hollywood's lead. Now that you've proved your point that there would be no United States without Abraham Lincoln, that foreign languages should be taught in elementary school, or that the most important person in your life was a bank teller, take that extra step and assure your reader that what she just read affects not just the present but the future as well. You rarely need to craft more than a sentence or two, but those post-production sentences can make the difference between an essay that simply ends and an essay that leaves a lasting impression in your reader's mind.

What does Hollywood draw on to make its memorable endings?
Here are some time-tested techniques:

- Paint a picture. *Avatar* ends this way. Jake's avatar lies lifeless
  until the very last moment, then opens its eyes. We are left
  hanging on an image of two eyes staring out at us. *Sleepless
  in Seattle* ends with imagery, this time with Sam and Annie
  walking away holding a teddy bear. *Dr. Strangelove* ends
  with Slim Pickens riding a nuclear bomb down to its target, an image that predicts self-destruction as the ultimate
  reward for those who attach themselves to war.

- Reprise the opening. The final scene of *Bucket List* appears
  to be a replay of the opening scene. A lone figure climbs a
  snow-covered mountain and buries an urn of ashes. The film
  ends as it began, until we learn that the figure at the end is
  Edward Cole's assistant carrying out his boss's last wishes.
  The ending offers us a future in which everything is as it
  should be. The issues brought up at the beginning of the
  film have been, no pun intended, laid to rest.

- Unravel a mystery. In the final scenes of *The Usual Suspects,*
  Roger "Verbal" Kint sheds his trademark limp as he walks
  down the street. Instantly, we know the true identity of the
  mysterious Keyser Soze, and we know he's still free to ply his
  trade.

Now that you know some Hollywood secrets, here are ways to use
them in your essay:

- Use a visual image as your picture of the future. Suppose
  your thesis is that a vigorous press is the best defense
  against a corrupt government. You might end by writing,

"Even a lone reporter can climb the steps of the Capitol and replace the For Sale sign with one that reads 'Open for the People's Business.'"

- Reprise an opening by borrowing some imagery, description, facts, or even phrases or sentences from the first paragraph of your essay and using them in your conclusion. If your thesis states that texting promotes education through the sharing of ideas, you might begin your essay by writing "Some people believe a pair of thumbs moving rapidly over a small keyboard has become the greatest threat to education since the invention of ditching." After you sum up your argument and demonstrate how you proved your thesis, you could conclude by reprising your opening and writing, "Rather than posing a threat, those pairs of thumbs moving rapidly over small keyboards are spelling out a new way of improving education."

- Conclude your essay by unraveling a mystery you created by withholding information. This is risky in academic writing. Hiding a key element of your argument until the last sentence will at best weaken your argument and at worst destroy it. On the other hand, when writing a personal essay (for example, a college application personal statement), the technique can serve you well. Imagine writing about someone who taught you an important lesson. You might withhold that person's identity until the end, especially if the person you are writing about is ... you. Most students write about lessons learned from parents, teachers, or relatives— so keeping your own identity secret until the last moment could add a nice surprise to your story, as well as predicting that, in the future, you'll be your own best advisor.

Like Hollywood filmmakers, you can prolong the story in your essay by showing your reader that what you wrote doesn't stop with the final period. That way, you'll always write a conclusion worth reaching.

Post a reply: _____

_____

_____

_____

On Location in Mary Land

"I'm looking for those moments I feel are going to make the film even better," says veteran film editor J. D. Ryan. "It's those moments that make a film a little bit more heartfelt, suspenseful, or exciting." More often than not, those moments come in the form of an image—a glance, a look, a flicker of an eyebrow, a gesture, or a pose.

It's images that make your essay heartfelt, suspenseful, or exciting, too. Ryan has images on film to work with. You have words on paper (see "Picture This," page 53). During post-production, Ryan's job is to make sure the images that capture a moment make it into the film. During your post-production you need to make sure that the words that capture an image make it into your essay.

To see how to do it, we need to take a little trip. Cut to …

Here we are in sunny Mary Land, home of … well … Mary. Last night, everyone was at Mary's house. There was supposed to be a party, but when the guests arrived, Mary wasn't around. We were hanging out in the living room, admiring the furniture, and then:

Mary came into the room.

Stop right here. Our missing hostess has mysteriously appeared. This is an important visual moment. Describe Mary. Write down her description. You have 10 seconds. Do it now.

Okay, time's up.

Moments later, Mary left the room. Everyone was wondering where she went until, without warning:

Mary skipped into the room.

Another important visual moment. Once again, describe Mary. You have 10 seconds. Describe her hair color, eye color, hairstyle, clothing, height, weight, body type.

Once more Mary vanished, but in a little while:

Mary danced into the room.

You can guess what's coming. Describe Mary. Her hair, eyes, and outfit. Don't laugh. It's her place. She can wear whatever she wants.

Here's what probably happened while you mulled over Mary. After the first sentence, your image of Mary was quite sparse. Female may have been the best description you could muster. Accurate, though hardly inspired.

You had better luck with the second sentence, when Mary skipped into the room. Mary had blond or red hair. She probably wore pig-tails or a ponytail. She was young and energetic. Her dress, more than likely, was blue. She might have had freckles.

Your results with the third sentence were equally detailed. Mary might have been more slender than when she was skipping, and maybe she was dressed in a tutu with pink shoes and dark hair, but she certainly cut a figure in your mind.

Even if your images of Mary were different, the chances are that after the first sentence you had virtually no idea what Mary looked like. If you were looking to make a moment out of Mary's entry, the first sentence would be akin to an editor having a few fuzzy frames of Mary to work with. The second and third sentences, the ones that created detailed mental pictures of Mary, are akin to an editor having solid raw material to work with. If you examined the sentences, though, they were almost identical. From the first to the second to the third, the sentences differed only in a single word.

That must be some word.

The difference lives in the verbs. Simply changing the verb changed the sentence from five image-free words to a five-word sentence that projected a lifelike version of Mary onto your brain. Therein lies the difference between strong and weak verbs.

"Came" is a weak verb. The word tells you little more than that at some point in time Mary was not in the room but later she was. "Came" conveys little information about Mary because the verb creates no visual image. It's as if a director shot Mary in the shadows. All you have of Mary is a vague impression.

"Skipped" and "danced" are strong verbs that create visual images. Both words convey Mary's passage from outside to inside the room, only they do so in a way that moves Mary out of the shadows and into the light. You were able to see a picture of Mary that fit your criteria for someone skipping or dancing into a room. One of the coolest parts, though, is that the Mary most people see, judging from the results in workshops, is darn near universal.

As one student pointed out, the best part is that Mary doesn't exist. She's just five words on a page. Yet you and countless other people reading this post can describe her skipping along, pigtails or ponytail flying behind her. And Mary doesn't exist.

Such is the power of strong verbs.

Once you're in post-production, perhaps the single biggest step you can take to improve your writing—any kind of writing—is to make those moments, as Ryan calls them, by using strong verbs to create vivid images in the minds of your readers. The second biggest step you can take is to use strong adjectives (see "How Shall We Dress This Noun," page 169). If you change nothing else about your writing but your choice of verbs, your writing will become noticeably more effective.

In Mary Land or wherever you write.

Post a reply: _____

_____

_____

_____

How Shall We Dress This Noun

Even if you're not a big fan of the *Star Wars* movies, you are undoubtedly impressed by their costumes, makeup, and props. The Empire's war ships, with their portholes, hatches, and appendages, look evil just by being. Darth Vader in an Armani suit instead of helmet and cape? Stylish, but hardly threatening.

George Lucas, the patron saint of *Star Wars,* is a stickler for details because he knows that what his actors and props look like conveys so much of the *Star Wars* mythology. A generic style would have saved him time and money, but Lucas wasn't interested in telling his story with robots made of cardboard boxes, mailing tubes, and aluminum foil. If clothes make the man, to trade on an old saying, costumes, makeup, and props can make the movie.

In writing, as in film, audiences form their first impressions of people and things from appearances. Think of adjectives (and adjectival phrases) as the makeup, costumes, and props of your essay. Like strong verbs (see "On Location in Mary Land," page 165), strong adjectives create mental images. Weak adjectives don't. While directors have to make their costume choices before shooting begins, writers are more fortunate. We can make necessary wardrobe changes during post-production.

Take the common description "a lot," as in, "I have a lot of homework." What is "a lot"? It's a piece of land without a house on it. A lot does little to tell your reader how much homework you're talking about.

Let's recast the sentence and dress up "homework": "I have a pile of homework the size of Mount Everest."

Get the picture now?

That's some serious homework. Chances are, as that image of homework entered your head, your eyes—at least your mind's eye—followed that pile of homework all the way up to the sky. (If Mount Everest didn't work for you, try substituting the highest point in your area—a mountain, a building, or a landmark.)

Along with expressions such as "a lot," two words that won't win any awards for costume or design are "very" and "really." What, exactly, is the difference between being sick and really sick? Once you're sick, tacking on a weak word doesn't change your condition. On the other hand, you could be gut-wrenchingly sick or deliriously sick or ghostly white sick. Each one dresses up "sick" in a different outfit. The same thoughts apply to "very." No one can see a person who's very hungry, but everyone can see a person who's compulsively hungry, violently hungry, or indiscriminately hungry.

The process of dressing up your nouns begins with seeing a mental picture of what you want your reader to see (see "Picture This," page 53). If you start with an image, you'll almost automatically veer away from weak adjectives because you can't see weak adjectives to begin with—and the adjectives you do use will fit your nouns as if they were tailor made.

Post a reply: _____

_____

_____

_____

Strong Nouns

This topic seemed to fall somewhere between being specific (see "Specific Is Always Better Than General," page 55) and choosing strong verbs and adjectives (see "On Location in Mary Land," page 165; and "How Shall We Dress This Noun," page 169), so it wound up with a post of its own.

There are moments in films that just call for a close-up. We all want to see the villain sweat under intense interrogation from a detective or an unrelenting cross-examination from a defense attorney. We want to see the look on a mother's face when she first holds her newborn baby or the tear in the eye of the hard-boiled hero when he stares at a picture of his long-lost love.

During post-production, it's time for directors and editors to decide just how close to the action they want the audience to be. Like you, they exit the production phase with lots of coverage (see "Coverage," page 79). In the editing room they create the desired image by selecting from close-ups and wide shots. You'll make your choice by selecting the appropriate nouns.

Just as verbs and adjectives can create images, so can nouns. Nouns, however, are the close-ups of writing. Compare:

Yesterday Mike had lunch.

with:

Yesterday Mike had a sandwich.

From the first sentence, you know Mike ate, though you probably have no idea where—at home, in a restaurant, on the beach, at a picnic, standing over the sink. It's as if Mike is a tiny little dot on the big screen. You can see him eating, but that's about all. After the second sentence you probably have a better picture of Mike at lunch. He ate with his hands. Lunch was probably a casual affair. Chances are he ate sitting down. We can do better, though.

Yesterday Mike had a pastrami sandwich on rye for lunch.

We're getting closer. Now you can probably see the sandwich (did you notice it was on rye bread?) and maybe where Mike ate it (a restaurant—perhaps a deli).

If Mike's lunch were described by:

Yesterday Mike had a pastrami sandwich that was full of sand.

You might even see Mike eating at a picnic or on the beach. The combination of strong, specific nouns (and a few well-chosen adjectives) turned Mike's lunch from far away to close up—not to mention from bland to interesting.

If only Mike could do that when he cooked.

Post a reply: _____

_____

_____

_____

Avoid Generalizations

There's a great old western called *Stagecoach*. Directed by a master of the western film genre, John Ford, *Stagecoach* was released in 1939 and stands today as a classic example of how to tell a story about the American West without special effects or a lot of clichés.

Ford opens the film with a wide, sweeping shot of the American plain, all sand and sagebrush. Even in black and white the view is compelling in its grandeur. To 1939 audiences, accustomed to black and white photography, the effect must have been riveting.

Given the punch of that panorama, you might wonder why Ford didn't shoot the whole film with panoramic vistas. The answer is, wide shots provide a general view of a scene at the expense of intimacy. The opening scene of *Stagecoach* shows us the world the story occupies, but the image includes so much that it's not clear to us, as viewers, what's important to look at. A film without those specifics would be difficult to watch. We'd see a stagecoach or a town and hear voices drifting in from nowhere with no idea who was speaking. Like close-ups (see "Strong Nouns," page 171), wide shots have their place in films. Used sparingly, they can add drama to a film. Used carelessly, wide shots can destroy a film's intelligibility. Directors and editors rely on the coverage (see "Coverage," page 79) to provide wide and close-up views of a scene. During post-production, they make the final choices about when to go for sweep and superficiality or depth and details.

Those are choices you have to make, too—only your choices are between specifics and generalizations.

Generalizations are the wide shots of essay writing. Used sparingly, generalizations create a sense of time, mood, tone, and place. Used carelessly, they undermine all your efforts to convince your reader of the validity of your point of view.

While you are building a carefully constructed case, your skeptical reader is looking for a way to punch a hole in your argument and walk away from your essay with mind unchanged. By generalizing, by claiming "Everybody knows …," "As we can all see …," or "It happens all the time …," all your reader has to do is find (or imagine finding) one person who doesn't know, who can't see, or to whom it hasn't happened and everything in your essay is instantly tainted with doubt.

"If he's wrong about this," your reader thinks, "can I trust anything else he says?" Hear that hiss? It's the sound of the air going out of your argument.

"But wait," you say, "this IS something everybody knows." Perhaps. Perhaps you've found that one fact in a gazillion that's universal. In that case, why state it? Everybody knows it. Save yourself the effort and words.

Can generalizations be used to good advantage in essays? Yes, if you're using them not to prove a point but, as wide shots are used in film, to establish a mood, setting, or tone.

You might start your essay with, "In all the world there is no place lonelier than Antarctica." Is it true? Who knows? People have their own ideas about what loneliness is. The sentence is there to establish the mood of the continent, not argue that Antarctica is the loneliest place on the planet. You're setting up your essay with your wide shot.

Now switch to your close-up lens and tell the story in detail.

Post a reply: _____

_____

_____

_____

What the Hero Didn't Do

In the film *Julie and Julia,* Julie Powell, one of the main characters, decides to devote a year to cooking every recipe in Julia Child's famous cookbook (well, it's famous to your parents). At the same time, Julie decides not to buy a designer gown, adopt a tiger, visit Istanbul, or train to become a Flamenco dancer. But the film isn't about any of that. The film isn't about what she didn't do, the film is about what she did.

It is hard, if not impossible, for a movie to show a not. Try photographing a person not sleeping. What would you see? A person walking around the house? A person driving a car? A person shopping for food? None of those are images of someone not sleeping. They're images of someone walking, driving, or shopping.

Describing a not in writing is deceptively simple. We can describe a swimmer as not too tall instead of short or a political candidate as not too bright instead of ignorant. The use of "not" makes the description sound dramatic. However, describing a person as "not tall" doesn't create that all-important visual image. Just how short is "not tall"? While it's easy to write the word, "not" is hard to visualize.

As you move your essay through post-production, pay attention to how you describe people, objects, and events. Think of yourself as a director and imagine you have encountered your description in a script. Can you convert that description into something audiences can see on the screen? If not, rewrite it. Here are some practice sentences to get you in the flow. Each one requires the reader to imagine a negative. Take a few minutes and turn these sentences around so they are about something instead of about not something.

- I didn't enjoy Shakespeare's *A Midsummer Night's Dream*.
- In World War II, Hitler wasn't looking to plunder new lands for gold and silver.
- I didn't like the way I spent my summer vacation.

When you have your own rewrites, take a look at some student examples:

- Halfway through *A Midsummer Night's Dream*, I started dreaming, too.
- *A Midsummer Night's Dream* left me counting the days until autumn.
- For Hitler, eliminating people he deemed imperfect was worth more than all their silver and gold.
- My summer vacation fizzled like a cheap birthday candle.
- My summer vacation was slightly more fun than a train wreck.

What were your rewrites like? Did they do what these examples did? Did they give your reader something to imagine? Can you see how, in your role as director, you could visualize what to film? A person sound asleep during a play or pulling pages off a calendar (or marking X's on the wall of a prison). Hitler herding people into concentration camps. A sputtering candle on a birthday cake, shooting sparks and wax in all directions. A train wreck right in the middle of Camp Cayuga.

Give your reader something to imagine and you'll never leave her tied up in nots.

Post a reply: _____

_____

_____

_____

Dancing in Place

It's not uncommon for an editor to cut together a sequence only to find, after letting his work sit for a day or two, he's created an awful moment when the film feels as if it's dancing in place.

Dancing in place occurs when the action in a movie repeats itself, bringing the story to a crashing halt.

Tired, bruised, and dripping wet after escaping from the alien death ray, the ancient Mayan bladed ball of death, and two furious ex-wives, our hero and his lovely heroine enjoy a moment of quiet on the banks of the river.

HERO: It sure is peaceful here.

HEROINE: Yes, it is.

HERO: Peaceful.

HEROINE: And quiet.

HERO: Yes. Quiet, too.

HEROINE: It's interesting that it's both peaceful and quiet.

HERO: At the same time.

HEROINE: And both at the end of an exciting day.

HERO: A very exciting day.

HEROINE: I meant that. I've never seen so much excitement in one day.

At this point we're ready to reach into the screen and strangle the next character who says "beautiful," "exciting," or "at the same time." We figured it out. They're alone. They have a moment's peace. That took four seconds. Now it's time to stop talking and start acting. Kiss each other. Have an argument. Fight off a zombie that wields an iPod as a martial-arts weapon. Anything to get the story moving again.

Keep in mind that people expect from essays what they expect from movies: a forward-moving journey. When your essay dances in place, you infuriate your readers the way such a movie infuriates its audience. As you review your essay, trim out the dancing in place—the restatement of the same thoughts, ideas, or arguments. Make sure each support point moves your reader forward on the journey from thesis statement to conclusion.

Keep your essay moving, and it will be beautiful and exciting. At the same time.

Post a reply: _____

_____

_____

_____

Coming Up Short

One filmmaker whose work is always a hit in college classes is Mel Brooks. Although he's a mid-twentieth-century artist, his brand of humor—at once silly and sophisticated, outlandish and satirical—continues to resonate well with film students. Brooks excels at all aspects of comedy, but one of his strongest areas is timing. Watch a Brooks film and you feel as if you're being pelted with humor. It's bam, bam, bam and then, when you're sure he's wrung every laugh he can out of the moment, bam, he hits you again. Brooks's success lies in his efficiency. He wastes little time setting up his jokes. Over his nearly 60 years as a comedy writer, performer, and filmmaker, Brooks has learned an important lesson about brevity.

So should you.

Audiences not only lose the logic of a joke as the time between the setup and the punch line grows longer, they also assume that the longer the time, the bigger the payoff will be. Spread out the beginning and end of a joke far enough and it's almost impossible to satisfy anyone. When working in the editing room, you can be sure that Brooks takes out every unnecessary frame between the setup and punch line of every one of his jokes.

You may not be playing your essay for laughs, but the rule of brevity still applies. The longer it takes for you to make your point, the more you risk losing the attention of your reader. You want to use all the words you need to be persuasive and no more.

Contrary to what you might have heard, brevity doesn't always mean wholesale pruning of your work. Comedy filmmakers know that humor is often made or destroyed in fractions of a second.

In an essay, the holding or losing of your reader's attention can come down to a handful of words.

Wordiness usually lurks in two places. One favorite haunt is multiple takes. During production you may have written the same description several times. Often, this repetition remains in subsequent versions because it's mistaken for emphasis. It's not.

Take the earlier sentence, "Filmmakers know humor is often made or destroyed in fractions of a second." In an earlier draft that thought was, "Filmmakers know humor is often made or destroyed in the smallest of moments. While the whole structure of the film needs to be designed for comedy, humor can be won or lost in fractions of a second." These two sentences convey the same idea. Multiple takes like this are easy to spot and even easier to fix. One take has to go, or the best parts of the multiple takes need to be merged together. Which approach you choose is up to you. Here the phrase "Filmmakers know humor is often made or destroyed" wound up merged with "fractions of a second" because the latter seemed more visual than "the smallest of moments." The result, "Filmmakers know humor is made or destroyed in fractions of a second" is a punchy, visual description that makes the point without wasted words.

Another hiding place for wordiness is adjectival phrases. When you see descriptions such as "the color of the book" instead of "the book's color," or "in the game I played in yesterday" instead of "in yesterday's game," or "the car with the dented fender on the right side" instead of "the car with the dented right fender," now you know what to do.

Under some circumstances wordier descriptions might add a degree of importance to a sentence or fit nicely with the rhythm of your essay. Most of the time, though, the extra words only call attention to the fact that they're unnecessary.

Trim those extra words. They're nothing to laugh at.

Post a reply: _____

_____

_____

_____

Too Much Description

Every now and then there's a film with sets and special effects so lavish that they rate their own dressing room with a star on the door. Often this star status is well-deserved because the sets and effects serve to cover up a lame story. While audience members are being dazzled by the images, they miss the fact that the plot has holes in it large enough for a pregnant Humvee on steroids to pass through.

Yes, that's right. A pregnant Humvee on steroids. See, it's possible to go for the dazzle factor in essay writing and achieve equally garish results. You can wind up with an image that, while spectacular, detracts from the point you're arguing or one so jarring it brings your argument to a halt. If the image is too fantastic, you run the risk of damaging the credibility of your argument as well.

During post-production, take a tip from the Hollywood pros and make sure you're not zooming in on lavish excess at the expense of solid storytelling.

When using strong visual images, use the fewest details you need to create the image in your reader's mind. Part of the pleasure of reading comes from the reader contributing details from her own imagination. You'll find "a stout tree with dense, green foliage" works better than "a tree, 19 feet tall, with two dozen branches, each containing a mass of green leaves as thick as bees in a hive." The latter may be technically correct, but the former will create the better image because it allows your reader to fashion one that most satisfies her.

Choose descriptions that strike your reader with impact, but don't hit her so hard you knock her senseless.

Post a reply: _____

_____

_____

_____

How to Score

Have you ever seen a silent film? A real silent film? One with no sound at all? Probably not. Even the films we call silent, such as the works of Charlie Chaplin, Buster Keaton, and D. W. Griffith, were (and still are) presented with a musical accompaniment. The music was so important to the presentation that studios often commissioned composers to create unique scores for the films; in larger theaters, those scores were performed by full orchestras.

Even in the sound film era, the musical score is a critical storytelling tool. The right musical performance is as important in post-production as the right acting performance is in front of the camera. The battles scene from *Star Wars* or the underwater scenes from *Jaws* would be little more than YouTube curiosities without John Williams's score energizing the action and heightening the drama. The rising crescendos; the uncomfortable minor chords; the racing strings; and the somber, plaintive woodwinds all amplify the emotions of the characters and the audience. If music is so important to the telling of a film's story, why not harness its power in your essays?

That doesn't mean you should write your essays on those greeting cards that play disco tunes from the '70s. What you're going to borrow from film scores is the principle of pacing. Like music, writing has a tempo and rhythm. Like films, if that tempo and rhythm remain at a single level, your reader's attention will drift and his sense of your writing will be anything but compelling. Time to switch hats again. Don one that puts you in a musical mood while you read these suggestions for adding your own literary score during post-production:

- Read your essay out loud (see "Word of Mouth," page 189) to get a sense of its rhythm.

- To pick up the pace of your essay, break longer sentences into shorter ones.

- Successive short sentences add drama and urgency. Compare "I entered the room and looked around, finally spying a cell phone on the table. I crossed the room, picked up the phone, and slid it into my pocket," with "I entered the room. I looked around. A cell phone was on the table. I crossed to it, picked it up, and slid it into my pocket." The short sentences and phrases create a sense of tension in the writing.

- To slow down the pace of your essay, combine short sentences into longer ones.

- Mix short and long sentences to vary the pace of your writing. When you speed up the tempo, consider slowing things down with a long sentence or two to allow your reader to catch her breath. If your pace is slow, a few short, quick sentences can perk up your reader's attention.

- The visual images you create (see "On Location in Mary Land," page 165; and "How Shall We Dress This Noun," page 169) affect the pace of your writing because your reader needs time to visualize the images. "The hillside came down in a flash," reads quickly because the image it creates goes by quickly. "The mud oozed slowly down the hillside," slows down the pace because it takes the reader a bit longer to visualize slowly oozing mud.

- Short words are like short musical notes. They quicken the pace. Long words, with multiple syllables, slow down the pace.

It's easy to vary the pace of your writing now that you know the score.

Post a reply: _____

_____

_____

_____

Word of Mouth

There will be times during post-production when you get so caught up in the details of your essay that you lose your connection with the journey you planned for your reader. While you're assembling your essay and fussing over word choices, commas, sentence lengths, and verb tenses, the flow of your essay silently slips away.

Film directors and editors face the same problem. As they assemble a film from shots that might last only a few seconds, it's easy for them to lose touch with what is literally the big picture. They solve their problem by periodically screening longer sequences of the film. These days, the majority of Hollywood films are edited on a computer, so a few keystrokes are all that's necessary for the editor and director to recapture their connection with the story.

You might believe screening your essay on a computer is the appropriate way to reconnect with your writing. The idea has merit, but it turns out there's a more effective method.

Read your writing out loud.

Writing may enter our brain through our eyes, but we pretend to hear the writing as if it's being spoken to us by that little voice in our head. (That might sound a little weird, but a similar process is at work when we watch films. Even though we know the characters in a film were photographed months ago on a sound stage, we pretend they're in the theater with us, performing the action right before our eyes. It seems we have to be a bit delusional to enjoy watching films and reading words.)

If your reader is going to hear your essay, then you need to hear it, too; and nothing beats hearing it the old-fashioned way—through your ears. Writing that sounds good when you hear it spoken will read well inside your reader's head. What are some things to listen for?

- If you stumble over words or phrases, fix them so you can read them smoothly.

- If a sentence is too long to read out loud, shorten it or break it up into smaller sentences.

- If what you're reading (whether the whole essay or only a part) feels repetitive in its rhythm, vary it (see "How to Score," page 186). One cause of repetitiveness is a large group of sentences with the same structure (typically subject-verb, subject-verb, subject-verb). Break up the repetitive feel by mixing up the sentence construction.

- If a word doesn't sound right or feel right in context, replace it with one that works. Even when a word is technically correct, it may not fit in your particular essay in that particular place.

- If a word, phrase, or sentence doesn't create the visual image that inspired it, change the word, phrase, or sentence until it does (see "I've Got a Question," page 46).

If you want your writing to speak to your reader, start by putting words in your mouth.

Post a reply: _____

_____

_____

_____

Test Screening

Film and television director Stephen Hopkins, who, in addition to directing a dozen or so films for movies and television, directed most of the first season of the television series *24*, tells this story about *24*'s pilot episode. "*24* introduced a new format of television show, and in the pilot you didn't find out until the very end that the story is about assassinating the president. Because we didn't show this up front, the way TV shows usually did, by the end of the episode the audience didn't care that much about what was going on.

"We reshot some things and in the split-screen opening added a character who says something about assassinating the president. The rest of the episode was almost the same. We showed it again and people loved it."

When Hopkins says, "We showed it again," he's talking about screening the episode in front of a test audience. A series of test screenings helped save the *24* production team from airing the pilot to what would have been at best a lukewarm reception.

Love them or hate them, test screenings are a familiar stop along the Hollywood film development route. The screenings allow studios to make changes to a film before it's released. These changes range from re-editing scenes all the way up to reshooting whole sections of a film that flat out flunk the test. Not all test screenings produce solid hits, and all anyone knows for sure is writers, producers, and directors will debate the value of a test screening long after the film in question has made its way to the DVD discount rack.

While Hollywood mulls over the merits, it's not a bad idea to give your essay a test screening. After working intensely on an essay, it's easy to imagine details in your work that aren't there. Passages you interpret quite clearly have different meanings to a reader encountering them for the first time. Giving your essay a test screening isn't a way to find out what you should have written, it's a way to make sure readers understand what you did write—or meant to write.

As with film screenings, one of the tricks for success (where success means a screening that provides feedback you can use to improve your work) is choosing the right audience. Studios usually know the targets for their films and express them in terms of demographics: males 12 to 18 years old, women 18 to 34 years old, and so forth. You, however, can be more selective.

When choosing your audience, take into account some of these suggestions:

- Pick small audiences. Three people ought to be enough. More than that and you could wind up with more information than you can use, most of it contradictory.

- Avoid parents and close relatives. They mean well but can be overcritical because they want your essay to be perfect or undercritical because they are afraid to dampen your spirits.

- Lay out the ground rules. Most people don't know how to give feedback on essays. Most writers don't know how to ask for what they need (see "Feeding Back," page 194).

- Choose an audience that's at the right level. When you write an essay for a school assignment, your ultimate reader is your teacher. Typically, though, you're expected to write for a mythical classmate, someone with your background and understanding of the topic. The easiest place to find your audience is in your class. Before you do, check with your teacher to make sure this type of peer review is acceptable. Remember, you also have friends outside your class and school.

Another important choice is your screening date. Your audience may take a few days to read and respond to your essay. Make sure you have enough time to absorb the feedback and act on it. Some feedback may prompt you to make a few simple edits. Other feedback might suggest the need for reshooting (or rewriting), so you'll want to allow time for pre-production (thinking about the changes and why and how you'll make them), production (drafting the changes), and post-production (editing and improving the changes). Plan accordingly.

Good, bad, or in between, feedback is nothing more than the opinion of the people providing it. On opening day, when you release your essay to the world, your writing has your name on it, and your test audience fades into history.

You are the final decision-maker. Use the feedback or lose it. The choice is yours.

Post a reply: _____

_____

_____

_____

Feeding Back

When studios hold test screenings for a just-out-of-post-production film (see "Test Screening," page 191), they first decide what kind of information they're looking for. No, they don't choose answers they want, but they do take care in choosing the questions. Asking a test audience, "Well, what did you think?" is as likely to elicit a shrug and a smile as it is an admission that half the audience members dozed off during the ending. After decades of testing, screening, re-editing, and testing again, studios have learned how to ask the right questions.

Most writers haven't. When they ask for feedback on their work, writers typically have no idea what feedback they want. If they're lucky all they'll get is a shrug and a smile. Usually, the results are far worse. Here's a simple experiment you can try to demonstrate the point. Take an ordinary object—let's say a house key—and ask a friend what he thinks of it. Chances are, you'll get one of three answers:

- I don't know.

- It's okay (or it's nice, or it's bent).

- What do you mean?

Now ask another friend if she can open a sealed box by using the key to cut the packing tape. This time you'll probably hear

- I don't know.

- Yes (or I suppose so).

- No (or I doubt it, I might damage the key).

Whatever the response, you say, "Why?" You'll get an explanation. It may or may not be the most scientific answer in the universe, but it will be an honest opinion of whether your friend thinks the key will work as an impromptu box opener.

The important word here is "work." You got a better, more useful, more detailed answer when you asked if the key was suitable for performing a specific task. That's what you want to know when you ask for feedback on your writing. Is your writing working? Does it convincingly argue your point of view?

Most people, however, don't know what writing is supposed to do. Asking them what they think of what you wrote is like asking them what they think of your house key. Their answers will focus on appearances rather than effectiveness, leading to responses such as "It's too long (or too short)," "It's funny," or "It's very good." While some of these responses may deliver a caffeine jolt to your ego, they're not useful when it comes to plugging holes and shoring up weaknesses in your work.

Fortunately, it's easy to get quality feedback from friends, teachers, or almost anyone (other than parents) if you first specify the use you have in mind. Here are questions my students have developed over the years to get specific, useful feedback from their readers:

- What parts of the essay hold your interest?

- Where does your attention drift?

- What in the essay would you like to know more about?

- Are there parts of the essay that make you think, "I couldn't care less"?

Without using the word, you are guiding your readers to tell you what parts of your essay work (hold interest and argue convincingly) and what parts of your essay don't. You just have to know how to ask.

And don't forget to say please and thank you.

Post a reply: _____

_____

_____

_____

Writing Is Rewriting

There will be times when sections of your essay won't work. Despite your rearranging paragraphs and choosing different verbs, adjectives, and nouns, the feedback from test screenings (see "Test Screening," page 191) will indicate something is wrong. That's when it's time to follow an old Hollywood axiom:

If you can't fix it, reshoot it.

Okay, the part about this being an old Hollywood axiom might be a little exaggerated. With all the money involved, producers and directors would walk barefoot across the Sahara to avoid reshooting. Yet even in Hollywood, there comes a time when filmmakers simply have to haul out the cameras and lights and rescue the movie.

One of these days you will have to rescue your writing.

When you do, the first thing to realize is that this is a normal part of the writing process. Rather than feeling discouraged, be thankful you found what's not working before your readers did, because now you're going to fix it.

The fix may require you to return to pre-production. Perhaps a support point is just plain weak—it lacks credibility. Do your research, draft a new support point, and run your rewrite through post-production, bringing your new scene's image-making power and conviction to the level of the rest of your essay.

Perhaps your opening no longer seems to set up the rest of your essay. It lacks excitement, mystery, or the promise of an interesting journey. Did you check the last paragraph of your current draft? If you read the post "That All-Important Opening Scene" on page 74, you know it promised that where you find your opening sentence might come as a surprise.

Well, surprise.

You may find the last sentence of your essay makes the best opening. If so, congratulations. You've demonstrated the extent to which your writing style and subject knowledge have improved over the course of post-production. The writing process is one of discovery; and once you discovered what you were writing about you may have written it all down in a smart, concise sentence right there at the end of your essay.

At least it's worth a look.

If your conclusion makes a better beginning, fine. Move it up to the top, and draft an even better finish. While you're at it, double-check that conclusion. Does it still work? Does it drive home your point of view or does it feel like a letdown? Does it seem to deflate your essay? Now that you've polished and refined the body of your essay, make sure that conclusion shines as well. What served you well in production and the early parts of post-production may have acquired a dull finish that demands to be refreshed.

Lose the parts of your essay that no longer say what you mean. Rewrite those parts that say what you mean but don't say it well. Conventional Hollywood wisdom or not, it's better to reshoot your work than see it shot down.

Post a reply: _____

_____

_____

_____

If Only …

To close this book, I want to talk about a topic that's as much a part of the movies as celebrities and as much a part of writing as periods and commas. That topic is emotion, especially the emotions of fear, uncertainty, and doubt. Only this time, I'm not talking about the emotions found in films and essays but the emotions surrounding the creating of those works.

All directors, actors, and writers share those emotions, just as they all beat themselves up because they believe those feelings are unique to them. When I speak with students about these feelings, the conversation inevitably turns toward how things would be different if only …. If only they had more experience or more time to write. If only they'd been able to pick their own topic. If only …, because then all the fear, anxiety, and doubt would vanish and they'd be able to write.

If only they knew.

All those emotions are part of the writing process. Everyone who faces the blank page has them every time they write. Those feelings are like a brother or sister who torments you. There's no escape, so you might as well find a way of making peace. (Actually, it's worse than a bad sibling, because leaving home when you're 18 may get you away from your sibling, but those writing emotions will pack up and move with you.)

Even moviegoing won't allay those feelings; I'm not sure anything can. But the movies might help convince you that you can learn to live—and write—in spite of your doubts. Well, not the movies, exactly, but a close relation: a screenwriter named Shirl Hendryx.

Shirl began his writing career in 1949 and wrote scripts for many of the iconic shows in television's Golden Era. Ask your parents (or grandparents) about *Bonanza, Mission: Impossible, Hawaii Five-O*, and *Columbo*. Shirl had his typing fingers in all of them.

He's retired from the industry now, but he still writes for the theater and works at his craft every day. I interviewed Shirl and asked him to discuss, from his vantage point of 60 years of writing, the same topics and problems you may have discussed with your friends, teachers, or yourself.

If only you had 60 years of writing experience, would things be easier? You decide.

Jay: After writing all those screenplays, stage plays must come fairly easy to you.

Shirl: Writing is still very hard. I've done lots of things in my life. I've worked in factories; I've been in the merchant marine. Lots of things. And I can't think of any work more difficult to do than good writing.

J: Then why do you do it?

S: Writing is also one of the most rewarding things to me. When I get done with a piece, look at it and say, "You didn't do bad with that," that's a great feeling.

J: In television, you were hired to write a script for a particular show. What was that like?

S: The first thing is you come up with an idea, something that interests you, something you think is exciting, something you think other people will be interested in. Even though I had to work within the confines of the show, I started by finding something I'm interested in.

J: But what if you were given a specific assignment, like write an episode about a fire in the hills?

S: If you tell me I have to write about something for an assignment, say a fire in the hills, and I have to come up with something, then I have to start thinking, "How can I use that? How can I use a fire in the hills?" I don't really think of the fire. I'll start thinking about people. Stories are about people. Two human beings. I'll think, in some way or another, what happens if they're in a fire area? Or what happens if ... what if a woman is blind and she suddenly finds out she's in a fire area? You play with these things. You say, "Oh, that's no good. I'll do this." Maybe there's a fireman. But he's off last night and he's drunk and he has to rescue a little kid and he's in no shape to do it.

J: Why start with the people when your assignment is a fire in the hills?

S: The interest is in how people deal with situations. The fire sets up the tension. The story is how people deal with it.

J: Did you have to do much research?

S: If I knew the characters, maybe a little less. But I'd always have to study the show. If I were going to do a *Streets of San Francisco* [note: a popular police drama in the 1970s with Karl Malden and Michael Douglas], and we were going to have to rescue people from a fire in the hills, I'd look at pictures of San Francisco, see if I could find some areas that were hard to get to or maybe full of old houses so the fire could spread. What I'd really try to do is get the producers to send me to San Francisco for a week, but that never worked.

J: Then what?

S: I sketched. Very similar to what a painter does. I get a general idea and play with it and maybe that becomes something.

J: Play with it as in write it down?

S: Or in my head. I played with it as I walked the dog in the morning or did other things. I didn't write anything because I didn't know what I wanted to write yet.

J: So these little sketches become part of the whole piece.

S: (laughs) Seventy percent of what I wrote I didn't use.

J: How can you possibly work at a job knowing you're going to throw away most of what you're doing?

S: I find myself sitting down and writing what is exciting to me. I don't worry whether it fits. Some of the best stuff you write will not fit because it doesn't work when you eventually find out where you're going with it.

J: How do you find out?

S: The sketches. The playing with ideas. Eventually, something starts taking hold and saying, "This is kind of where you want to go." Then more of what you write fits.

J: But every day?

S: I think you have to go to the well every day, and a lot of times you come back with nothing. And you've got to get to the place where you don't hate yourself for coming back with nothing. You try something, you give it the effort, try it three or four ways, and wind up thinking, "This is awful. I tried to do it and the day is gone." Okay. The day is gone. The next day you may have four inspirations. You've got to go to the well.

J: So there's value just in the doing?

S: I find if you do the hard work of trying to lick something, all the while thinking it's not worth anything, some morning while you're showering, it will all come to you, and you'll think it's an epiphany. It's not an epiphany. If you hadn't put all that work in there, it wouldn't have happened. What you've done is release the anxieties. But it doesn't come out of nowhere. Only after all that work does it seem, "This is so easy. Why didn't I think of that before?" Only it isn't easy. That's why you work every day.

J: I understand you had writer's block.

S: I was blocked for three years. I couldn't write a thing.

J: That must have been frightening.

S: I was making a living from my writing and then one day it stopped. I didn't know how to get out of it. I could put something in the typewriter, I'd get three or four pages, and then it just wouldn't go. I just couldn't do it.

J: You didn't starve, and you're writing now, so something must have happened.

S: A friend of mine, a playwright, told me to get a dictating machine. It was the best thing I ever did. I started dictating my ideas. What's good about that is you aren't staring at your writing saying, "That's not quite right. Let me work on it." You're doing what actors do when they improvise. Letting it flow. First thing in the morning, I'd type up what I dictated the day before. And as I'm typing, I'm saying, "Whoa. Wait a minute. Do this." I was automatically beginning to do something … I was back in the writing process.

J: Do you still dictate?

S: I have a little recorder I carry in my pocket. When I walk in the hills very often I'll come up with those epiphanies again. I carry it with me all the time.

J: If you're dictating whatever comes to mind, it sounds as if you don't write in order.

S: What's exceedingly important is when you've got the idea, get it down now—because if you don't, when you come back to it four days later you won't get the magic, the passion. It's important to get it down while the fever is there. It may not be right, but at least it'll have the feeling.

J: What's the best way for someone to learn to be a better writer? Are there some books or exercises you'd recommend?

S: (laughs) Well, maybe your book. I don't know; I haven't read it. I'll tell you, though ... in all these years ... the only way I've found to learn about writing is to write. You give what you wrote to somebody to read and you find out, "Why aren't they getting what I want them to get? What is it I'm not doing? What is it I'm not conveying? Because I felt it." Then you write some more, and someone reads it, and you keep doing that until you're old like me.

I hope you heard in Shirl's words his deep love affair with writing. Nonetheless, he still approaches each writing day with the same anxiety and uncertainty as you. Perhaps you also heard in his words the story of a person who has found his writing process and who relies on it for the sustenance all writers need so they can one day look at what they've written and say, "You didn't do too bad with that."

You may not learn this in school. I hope you've learned it from this book.

And I hope to see you at the movies.

Index

J–K–L

P

Q–R

T